In All Seriousness....
Totally Funny Bible
Stories

Darnnell Reese

DEDICATION

This book is dedicated to my beautiful mom Cheryl for giving me life and for being the funniest (nonprofessional) comedian I know (after Katt Williams). Your sharp wit was what I drew upon. I pray I do not disappoint you, but nevertheless, you are the comedian in the family. I know I can <u>never</u> take that title:-) I love you mom!

To my sweet grandmother. Because you walked with God, He also shows love to and abundantly blesses a thousand of your generations that have come after you. Thank you so much for being an amazing example to our family. You have obediently trained us up in the Way that we should go and we shall <u>not</u> depart. Rest in paradise sweet Josephine.

And my loving husband and best friend Terrence. As always, you are my rock in this not always sunny or funny world. Thank you for unselfishly and habitually bringing love, laughter and sunshine to my life, every day. God Bless our marriage and give us long life together. Amen.

ORIGINS: EXCERPT FROM MY PRIVATE JOURNAL

December 12, 2017

Thank you so much Heavenly Father God Yahweh. Last night I experienced a great transformation of my mood. You gave me an infusion of grace and I felt so much better. Last night, you also put another book on my heart. A humorous book about all the funny things I laughed out loud about in the Bible. I really like what you put on my heart because I love to laugh, especially at things that are truly edifying and beautiful. Your stories and Your Word is life. In all my ways I want to bring glory and honor to you. In Jesus name I pray, Amen.

TABLE OF CONTENTS

Origins: Excerpt from my private journal iv

Table of Contents v

ACKNOWLEDGMENTS 7

1 Judgy Judah, Shamed and Out-Gamed By Tamar 8

2 Are We There Yet? And Other Exodus Misbehavin' 19

3 Jonah's Unwise Choices Were Bad for His Health and Others 39

4 Paul, Vicarious Demon Slayer and Deadly Orator 50

5 Saul, The Many Faces of Cray-Cray 60

6 Balaam or the Donkey, Which One is the Jackass? 69

7 Please Go Home Uriah and Sleep With Your Wife! 75

8 Nehemiah, Provoked To Slapping and Hair Pulling 81

9 Yo Widow, Imma Let You Eat, But Feed Me First 86

10 Elijah, Rundown and Burned Out 94

11 Samson: Pillow Talk with Two-faced Females Will Be Your Ruin 101

12 Wildfires, A Jawbone and Pillars: Weapons of Mass Destruction 108

13 People Hate When You Make a Scene For Jesus, But He Loves It 120

14 Jesus Sharpshooter of the Truth 125

ABOUT THE AUTHOR 137

References 138

Movie and TV Guide, Enjoy! 146

Darnnell Reese

ACKNOWLEDGMENTS

Thank you to my loving in-laws Joe and Annie (rest in peace). Your love and kindness have blessed me in so many ways. I appreciate you so much. You have always been wonderful to me, and I thank God for blessing me with you. I love you with all my heart.

Thank you Deidra, you are my heart. Your honesty and encouragement are everything to me. May God continue to keep you, bless you abundantly and shine His face upon you.

Thank you family, extended family, and friends who provided their generous and gentle support in my writing endeavor. It is so truly appreciated.

1 JUDGY JUDAH, SHAMED AND OUT-GAMED BY TAMAR

Judah was one of Jacob's (later renamed Israel) twelve sons. Israel had two wives, Leah and Rachel, plus their mistresses, who also bore him children. Judah came from Jacob and Leah's union. The terms Jew and Jewish derive from his name.

For context: Judah and his three sons lived in Canaan—the same land his descendants would migrate to during the Exodus. Only after the Exodus did Canaan become known as Israel, once the Israelites expelled the previous inhabitants. The southern part was called the territory of Judah.

Judah's two oldest sons, Er and Onan, both married Tamar at different times, and both died, leaving her twice widowed. They did evil things God didn't like, so they were killed. Judah had one son left, a child named Shelah. He promised Tamar she could marry Shelah once he came of age.

My sincerest apologies—as confusing as this sounds, it's about to get more confusing. But I promise, I'm about to land this plane. There was a tradition for the surviving brother to marry the deceased brother's widow to carry on his name. This custom, called the Levirate marriage, wasn't handed down by God at this point. Adding to the confusion, "Levirate" sounds like it derives from Judah's brother Levi—the one associated with Levitical priests, Levitical laws, and the Book of Leviticus. Moses and Aaron were Levi's descendants. Easy to misconstrue.

Here's where my mind twisted into a pretzel: how do you pass down an ancient tradition named after someone who's still alive? My mind was blown to smithereens for nearly three minutes—until I Googled "Levirate custom" and found the truth. Fret not! Our biblical knowledge is intact. "Levirate" comes from Latin and means "husband's brother." It has zero to do with Levi. At this point in the Bible, Jacob was alive and well, so God's promises to him hadn't been fulfilled yet. No Moses, no Exodus, no Mosaic Law. A law similar to the Levirate custom became God's sovereign word later in Deuteronomy 25:5-6. Whew! Had I not researched this, you wouldn't be reading this book. Talk about crisis averted!

Hopefully you're still with me. Now we can get back to spilling the tea about Judah and Tamar.

See, what had happened was: once the older son Er died, Judah made Onan marry Tamar to carry on Er's lineage. Onan probably didn't want to, but he obeyed his father. Then he sabotaged his own efforts to impregnate her. He knew their firstborn would technically be Er's child—his nephew-son, not his own. So Onan deceitfully ejaculated outside Tamar's body. Since he didn't do what was right, he was killed too. Tamar was twice widowed.

After Onan's death, Judah told Tamar to remain a widow and stay with her father until Shelah was grown. Here lies the problem with "Judgy" Judah. He was a stickler for rules, fairness, and appearances—but in this matter, he was insincere. "Remain a widow" in Genesis 38:11 sounds like Tamar had the option to remarry if she chose. Judah was essentially saying, "Don't get married—wait for my son Shelah to grow up and marry him." By giving her those specific instructions, he bound himself by oath. But he took Tamar's options away with false hopes. Had he been honest—or better yet, bid her a heartfelt farewell—she could have remarried any other man. Instead, she felt obliged to wait. She never asked to marry Shelah. And Judah never intended to let his last son marry her anyway. In his mind, Shelah might die too if he married Tamar, as if she was cursed. Tamar probably thought *his* family was the accursed. The curse sentiments went both ways.

Because Judah never intended to give Tamar his last precious son, he kept feeding her excuses about why Shelah wasn't coming to marry her. Meanwhile, Tamar's ovaries weren't getting any younger, and Judah's inconsiderate fib may have cost her precious offspring. Barrenness—or the perception of it—was a very real fear for women in biblical times. A woman's social acceptance and household standing depended on her fertility. Uh-huh, that's right! Octomom would have been president of the Harper Valley PTA[1] back then. Without a Doubt[2], Tamar was shunned and judged by other women—especially those with a gaggle of kids.

Once Shelah had grown up and Judah still hadn't kept in touch, Tamar realized he was stringing her along. She made up her mind to take control of her fate and her fertility. Determined not to let anyone stop her from having a baby—not even her slick-talking father-in-law—Tamar devised a foolproof plan.

During this period, men would go sheep-shearing, an occasion of festivity—and often licentiousness. Licentiousness is a fancy way of describing the shenanigans typically observed during Bike Week in Myrtle Beach, spring break in Miami Beach, or "What happens in Vegas stays in Vegas." Let's just say men and women are not always on their best behavior. Tamar learned that Judah was heading to Timnah to get his sheep-shearing party on. His wife had recently passed, he was out of the mourning period, and all signs indicated Judah was about to get buck-wild.

Tamar devised an ingenious plan to trap him and get what she'd wanted from the get-go: a baby. She disguised herself with a veil over her face, resembling a prostitute, and waited on the road to Timnah. Strutting by with his freak flag flying, Judah fell right into her trap. At the sight of the mysterious Lady Marmalade[3], he propositioned her for her services. He had no idea he was about to get busy with his own daughter-in-law. Pretty sneaky, Tamar.

Not only was Tamar playing a shrewd game of chess—she was thorough. Before she let the old man romp with her, she asked what he'd give her for her time. Fast-talking Judah had nothing to offer but a promise to send a young goat from his flock. His word was unreliable, as we already know from the Shelah situation. Tamar realized she'd need verifiable evidence or Judah would go back on his word again. So she asked for his seal, cord, and staff as collateral. These items were personal and distinctive—as identifying as Judah's Sheep Herder's United ID card, his fingerprints, or his DNA.

Speaking of DNA, Tamar conceived during their encounter. She was so meticulous with her scheming that without even using an ovulation prediction kit, she calculated precisely when she'd be ovulating. Pure talent. Tamar was a Bad Mama Jama[4]!

Afterward, Tamar returned to her normal life and resumed wearing her widow's clothing. How sad that she was still in mourning clothes—all because jerk-around Judah kept dangling this phantom carrot in front of her. Like his daddy Jacob, Judah was a deceiver and trickster. The apple didn't fall far from the tree. But rest assured, Tamar had the last laugh.

Before we get to how things righteously unfurl, I'll give Judah credit for trying to send the promised goat. He asked his friend the Adullamite to take it to "the prostitute who works the road at Enaim." Judah wisely wanted his incriminating stuff back. Of course, he never found her because she wasn't an actual prostitute. Tamar was a woman on a mission to reclaim her blessings.

Within three months, Tamar's little bambino bump started showing. When word got back to pompous, pious Judah that his "ever-mourning" daughter-in-law was pregnant—and apparently a prostitute—he instantly sentenced her to death by incineration. What-the-what?! Judah was a patron of prostitutes, a customer of call girls, a pursuer of poonani, and a purchaser of poontang. Yet he severely judged her. Yep, Judah's smug, self-righteous face was next to "male chauvinist pig" and "hypocrite" in the first manuscript of the Hebrew dictionary.

As Judah's henchmen eagerly served Tamar her death warrant, she threw a monkey wrench at his smug head: "I am pregnant by the man who owns these." Looking at him side-eyed, she added, "Let me know if you recognize any of these items"—and handed over the seal, cord, and staff (Genesis 38:25). Game always recognizes game. Judah had no choice but to concede that Tamar was more righteous than him. He'd foolishly played mind games with her about Shelah, but now Tamar was not only with child—she was pregnant with twins! Winning and twinning!

Tamar gave birth to two healthy baby boys. During delivery, the midwife tied a scarlet cord around the wrist of the first baby who stuck his hand out. But when he drew it back in, the other baby made his escape first. The one who broke out first was named Perez; the one with the scarlet cord was named Zerah.

The final laugh? Perez was none other than the ancestor of our Lord and Savior Jesus Christ! Tamar, who was almost denied her dreams because of a know-it-all, puffed-up patriarch, became the matriarchal progenitor of the Messiah.

One lesson here: don't let anyone come between you and your dreams. God's got big plans for you if you're bold enough to take them. Another lesson: when our hearts are in the right place, God can make a miracle out of our messes. Judah's heart was in the right place when he obligated his sons to marry their dead brother's widow. He meant no harm and tried to do what he felt was right—but in this matter, it only made things worse. That doesn't mean we shouldn't do the right thing in tricky situations. Where there is no Malice[5] or ill will, God will make our crooked paths straight.

In a different Bible story, had it not been for "Judgy" Judah, his younger brother Joseph would have been killed by their jealous brothers. Egypt would have never stockpiled rations, and the great famine would have wiped out countless lives. But Judah did what he always tried to do: the right thing. He interrupted his brothers' murderous plans and spared Joseph's life. Joseph went on to save many lives and was the reason for the great Exodus.

Tab 1. Family Tree of Jacob/Israel & Judah and Tamar

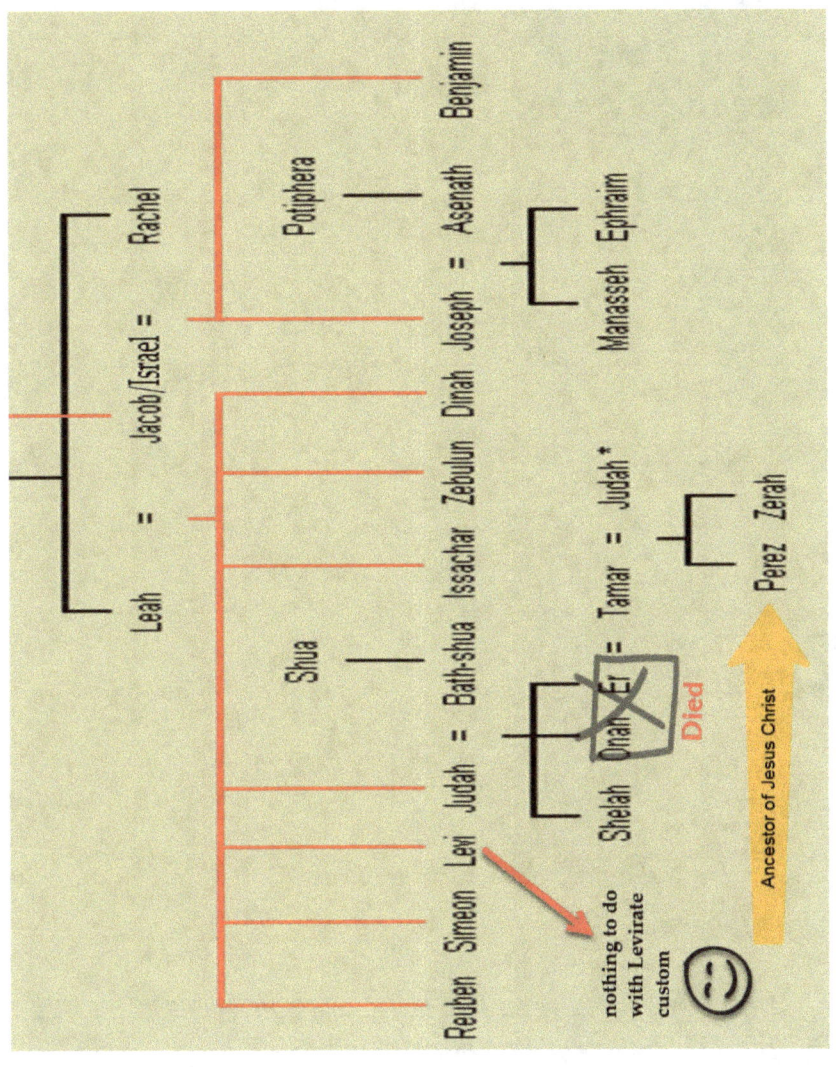

Table 1

Source: https://www.darkmirrors.org/genesis.php Accessed: 3/27/2018

Map 1. Judah and Tamar's Encounter

Map 1. *Source http://www.bible-history.com/geography/ancient-israel-old-testament.html Accessed: 11/28/2017*

2 ARE WE THERE YET? AND OTHER EXODUS MISBEHAVIN'

If the thought of a family road trip with two, three, or five children and your pets brings on cold-sweat panic—or has you reaching for a belt, a switch, and an extra-strength Excedrin—you are not alone. Now imagine taking a road trip with more than 600,000 immature, undisciplined, contemptuous people with no respect for anyone or anything. And having sole responsibility for all their needs.

In the late '70s, my eldest uncle Louis attempted such a chore with me, my brother, and three of my cousins in his late-model woodgrain-paneled station wagon. With his one free hand, he tried to whip us from the front seat to the back with his long leather strap. All of us little rascals leaped seats trying to dodge his wild lashes, sidesplittingly laughing at his maniacal expressions of anger and rage. After all these years, I must sincerely apologize to my uncle Louis for our mischievous conduct, which caused him to momentarily lose his mind.

The book of Exodus tells a similar story—and explains why an eleven-day journey to Canaan took forty years.

The short answer: the Israelites tested God like Bébé's Kids[6]. If you've never heard this expression, here's the Urban Dictionary definition: "Bay Bay kids—kids who don't listen to their parents and throw fits in stores and act a fool in public. Anyone's kids can be a 'bay bay kid' regardless of race, gender or socioeconomic status." To be fair, the Israelites probably misbehaved because they had PTSD. Post-Traumatic Stress Disorder can be a byproduct of 400 years of bondage, abuse, and torture. It doesn't take an MD or PhD to understand how slavery can cause mental defects and deficiencies—and unfortunately, often manifests as lawlessness.

The exodus journey began because God, Jehovah Yahweh, finally freed the Israelites after 400 years of Egyptian oppression. Pharaoh didn't willingly set them free—he reneged on his word many times, repeatedly defying and insulting God Most High. By then, the Hebrews were so mentally beaten and broken that God had to provide them a strong, fearless leader to take them by the hand. Otherwise, Stockholm syndrome would have kept them in Egypt, ludicrously loving their life of captivity. God hand-selected Moses to represent the people and petition Pharaoh to let them go. Pharaoh said "Yes," then "No," then "Yes," then "No." Nauseating and nerve-wracking for the already jumpy Hebrews. On the verge of a nervous breakdown, they didn't know what to do.

Ultimately, God pummeled the Egyptians with ten plagues ranging from irritating to unequivocally deadly. Finally, the thrashed Pharaoh begged them to leave. But of course, wishy-washy Pharaoh came after them again. The Red Sea was parted, the trailing Egyptians were drowned, and the Hebrews were on their way to the land of milk and honey.

Now all they had to do was walk where God said to walk and do what God said to do. Yahweh provided for their every need. He covered them under a protective cloud of smoke and personally escorted them through the unknown wilderness. He lovingly gave them instructions through Moses—and even wrote many down. He provided ample food from the sky, called manna. All they had to do was obey! But they were their own worst enemy the entire way. One thing after another got them in trouble with Yahweh. Non-stop bellyaching and malicious complaining kept them in hot water with God.

From the time they left Egypt, they continuously lost heart and bitterly criticized Moses about every discomfort, challenging God by incessantly murmuring that they should have never left Egypt. How they rationalized going back to slavery being better than freedom with God is mind-boggling. Who would choose to stay a slave? Not most people. But this bunch tested not only Moses's patience—they would have tested Job's patience.

When God decided to move them to the Promised Land, He already knew it was a short trip. Bada-bing, bada-boom, and we're here. I'm certain God gave them the benefit of the doubt—*even these people could withstand an eleven-day journey*. Unfortunately, they couldn't. They were a multitude of miscreants, wailing and whining all day long.

These people caused God more grief than the girl in The Bad Seed[7] ever could. They complained about not having water at every pit stop. They complained about not having leeks and onions. They complained about not having meat in the cooking pots. They openly lamented the lack of variety in their daily meal—not only within earshot of Moses, but knowing God was present. Reverence for Jehovah Elohim was not high on their priority list because they were suffering from lack of fleshly delights. That God saved them from an oppressive tyrant was beside the point. Right then and there, they wanted what they wanted, and everybody was going to hear about it.

To show you how quickly a road trip can turn from sing-alongs to stone tablets being flung and smashed in anger, take a look at the events where the Hebrews lost their ever-loving minds.

The first hissy-fit happened only three days after leaving Egypt! They lost it because the water tasted funny. The Hebrews came upon an area where the water was bitter and foul, so they blamed Moses as if it was his fault. Instead of calmly explaining, "Hello Sir, I just wanted to inform you this water is putrid and stinky. Is there anything that can be done? Do you by chance have a refreshing Sprite or Fresca?" Instead, with the comportment of hateful heathens, they fumed at Moses. Fearing an uprising over the taste of water he had zero control over, Moses cried out to God. God told

Moses to throw a piece of wood in the water, which miraculously removed the bitter taste (Exodus 15:22). Problem swiftly solved—and a miracle to boot. You'd think the Hebrews would be encouraged, amazed, empowered at how awesome their God is. Yet they continued complaining openly, behaving obnoxiously and belligerently.

The next thing that incensed these impolite Israelites was manna—the food God rained down from heaven that tasted like wafers with honey. Yes, you heard right. They were peeved because God gave them heavenly nourishment. How insensitive of Him. In their immaturity, they expected all the accoutrements from Egypt: onions, leeks, garlic, meat, yada yada yada.

Didn't they know this wasn't a Royal Caribbean luxury cruise? It was a rescue mission from a hostile nation. Weren't they there at the harrowing escape when wicked Pharaoh tried to hunt them down? These toddlers didn't realize the more they misbehaved, the longer this road trip would be. Instead of being thankful, they harshly criticized Moses for the lack of menu options.

Moses was understandably distraught. With great patience and restraint, he informed the rowdy rug rats that God had heard their litany of complaints and would provide quail in addition to the manna. Every morning they'd have manna, and in the evening, quail (Exodus 16).

♪♫ *She'll be coming round the mountain when she comes...* ♫ For Pete's sake, here we go again. Circling back around the water mountain. I know—you probably can't believe I'm about to tell you they had more complaints about water, even after witnessing all those amazing miracles. Let's see: God parted water at the Red Sea. He turned bitter water to refreshing drinkable water. They should have realized God is the Water Whisperer. He knows how to handle any water crisis! All they needed to do was approach Moses in a dignified manner. Better yet, a reasonably smart person would deduce Moses already knew they needed water—he's a human being for goodness' sake. God was giving them everything they asked for in short order, so there was no need for tantrums. But no. These choleric crybabies kept poking the bear with their cranky attitude. They went so far as to say, "Why did you bring us up out of Egypt to die of thirst?!" Truly a churlish bunch. Moses cried out to God again because the people were so rude. God had Moses use his staff to strike the rock, and instantly fresh drinking water flowed. This third water miracle still didn't soften these stiff-necked people's cantankerous hearts (Exodus 17).

The next "Don't make me come back there" incident was what this impetuous brood did while waiting on Moses to return from speaking with God. They foolishly decided Moses was gone for good, so they fashioned an idol out of gold jewelry and worshipped it as their God who "brought them up out of Egypt." Adding insult to injury, they had a feast and celebratory orgy to honor this golden calf. All Moses's fault, of course, because he was taking too long. If not for Moses begging and pleading on their behalf, God would have literally destroyed these rebellious rascals (Exodus 32).

We Want Meat! We Want Meat! Here we go again—the people demand meat for the second time. They wailed: "If only we had meat to eat! We remember the fish we ate in Egypt at no cost—also the cucumbers, melons, leeks, onions and garlic. But now we have lost our appetite; we never see anything but this manna!" (Numbers 11:4-6).

Boy oh boy, these people were pure frustration to God and Moses. Who could tolerate their non-stop complaining? No one! To be fair, this could be the same incident previously mentioned in Exodus. But since the Hebrews were profoundly oblivious of God's miracles, this may be totally separate. God gave them quail before, and now they wanted more—maybe different meat. Simply asking God would have been wise. But in the fashion of spoiled, hangry kids who scream "We want McDonalds!" in the backseat, they verbally denounced God's manna. Angered at their lack of gratitude, God said, "OK, you want meat? I'll give you so much meat it will be coming out of your nostrils!" Then He sent flocks of quail that piled up all along the campsite. Before they could eat the heaps already landed, more quail flew in and landed on top. They didn't even have an opportunity to pluck the meat from between their teeth before those who had grumbled were dead. How? Because in addition to the mountain of meat, God sent a deadly plague afflicting all who craved it. He gave them something to really cry about— but sadly, they still didn't learn.

"Stop touching me!" "I'm not touching you!" "I'm telling!" Do these petty arguments sound familiar among troublesome children during long car rides? Think of the Hebrews as such. They were not mature in the least.

Now, Miriam and Aaron talked badly about their little brother Moses. Moses was so humble—he wasn't their problem. The siblings were jealous because he was married to a Cushite woman. They used that petty fact to talk behind his back, not discerning that God is always listening. Both said Moses wasn't the only one God spoke through. It sounded like they wanted in on more of the closed-door meetings Moses attended with God. But if that's what they wanted, they should have Taken[8] their concerns to God, who made all the decisions, not Moses. Because of their pot-stirring, God called all of them into a closed-door, butt-whipping session that got very ugly, very fast. God told them exactly what the lay of the land was. I visualize God as an old-fashioned mother, painfully pinching both Aaron and Miriam by their fleshy upper arms, and between tightly clenched lips, snarling:

> *When there is a prophet among you, I, the Lord, reveal myself to them in visions, I speak to them in*

dreams. But this is not true of my servant Moses; he is faithful in all my house. With him I speak face to face, clearly and not in riddles; he sees the form of the Lord. Why then were you not afraid to speak against my servant Moses? (Numbers 12:6-8).

After God scolded Miriam and Aaron up one side and down the other, He still wasn't finished. As He left in a cloud, Miriam received a hideous parting gift. All the siblings were Scared Straight[9] at the horrific sight of Miriam's white leprous skin. Moses and Aaron both fell face down to intercede for her. God healed her after seven days, but it was a valuable lesson to all who doubted how God felt about His servant Moses. So the matter shouldn't be brought up again, right?

Wrong. The matter was brought up again because these jokers were thick-headed. Korah, another angry agitator, irreverently spoke out against Moses, just like Miriam and Aaron had. Korah, a prominent Levite, and a few other high-ranking wannabes were jealous because Moses was God's prophet and spokesperson. They challenged Moses's authority: "We're holy men too.

Why should we only listen to you? You've taken yourself way too seriously. We can make our own decisions."

Moses tried to warn them—especially after seeing how God punished Miriam for the same foolishness—but they stubbornly disrespected him. So Moses invited all the disgruntled members to reconvene the next day and let the Lord decide who was holy and who God wanted as His representative. These agitators really made Moses angry with their ungodly rebellion and hurtful accusations. Moses had been nothing but kind to them, unlike how they were treated in Egypt. Now these problem children were throwing him under the bus with false accusations of overstepping his authority.

Enraged, Moses asked God not to accept their grain offering. He literally blocked their blessings. You know Moses was God's man if he could smack down prayers. Never had Moses been so angry as to petition God to reject their offerings. I don't think these belligerent rebels understood Moses was the only thing that saved their collective butts all those other times when God wanted to wipe them out and start over. It was because of Moses prostrating and pleading for their forgiveness that God allowed them to remain alive. After the golden calf incident, they all would have been grease stains on the pavement had it not been for him. And now they were egregiously lying on him.

Moses was right to become indignant. He told God, "I never took so much as a donkey from these people and they treat me like this" (Numbers 16:15). Unfortunately, Korah recklessly and foolishly did not repent before the next day's meeting. When God showed up, He put a permanent end to that argument. He granted Moses his request to not accept their offering. When Korah and his crew presented sacrificial incense, God's earth opened wide and swallowed Korah, his buddies, their closest kinfolk, and their belongings. The rest of the Hebrews scattered so they wouldn't be devoured too. With such a grand spectacle, you'd think the rest would be on their best behavior from then on. Right?

Wrong. They instantly started in on Moses, saying it was his fault the people were swallowed up. Didn't they just see what God did to those other rebels? Why would they do such a stupid thing?! One can only surmise they were truly senseless and cruising for a bruising. At once, a deadly plague wiped out all those who spoke against Moses. They were begging for a beating. God gave them what they wanted—something to really cry about! But they still hadn't learned. If not for Aaron standing between the living and the dead with an incense offering, the plague would have taken more than the 14,700 who perished. Adding the 250 who died with Korah, it's clear all those insolent Israelites were slain as punishment for non-stop rabble rousing.

When God ultimately gave them the green light to take possession of the Promised Land, would you believe they found reasons to complain about that? Before I get to those new gripes, let me show you how much of a pain these Israelites were.

Before setting foot into the Promised Land, they had to spy it out to make sure it was safe. This indicates serious lack of trust in Yahweh. They didn't feel safe going in until they inspected the land—as if God was setting them up. To appease them, Moses selected twelve prominent men, one from each tribe to scout out the land God was graciously giving them. When the spies went up to peek at the new land, they saw it was good, flowing with milk and honey—a colorful way of saying lush and abundantly fertile. They saw grapes so big they had to carry them on a pole with a man holding each end. All this goodness was theirs for the taking. Nothing could stop them because God was with them, right?

Well, they were their own worst enemy. They came back and gave the most alarming, paralyzing report. The land was overrun with giants and devoured its inhabitants. They claimed they couldn't take this land from the current bloodthirsty inhabitants. Not that they were lying—but they failed to acknowledge how God was with them. He had been trying since Egypt to show them His awesome might, His all-knowing, His all-powerfulness. Miracles upon miracles. How could they keep ignoring all He was doing?

God was fed up. Because of their constant distrust and rejection, He rescinded His invitation to all those stiff-necked people. For the record, the rudest thing a person can do is be ungrateful toward someone bending over backwards for them. And that's what these ornery objectors did the entire trip. They didn't deserve His good gift. He sentenced them all to die right there in the wilderness, within sight of the Promised Land. After forty years, God allowed only Joshua and Caleb from the older generation, plus all their offspring, to enter His peace and rest in the good land. He waited forty years so all the negative naysayers were good and dead.

As usual, the Israelites realized they'd made a boo-boo by being so distrusting and hesitant. After all their paralyzing anxieties and over-analyzing God's good gift, now they were gung ho: "Let's go and take the land our God has given us!" But it was too late. God wasn't changing His mind. At this news, they had the audacity to furiously rise up against Moses and Aaron again. Not only did they threaten to stone the leaders, they stupidly declared they'd elect a "new leader" to take them back to Egypt. Remember, their favorite song was "Why did you take us out of Egypt to die?" This was the last straw. As a result of this latest rebellion and the ten prior acts of defiance, God told them all they'd be forced to live in the desert until every last grouchy grumbler died there. Only their children would enter the good land He promised.

♪♫ Here we go round the mulberry bush—the mulberry bush—the mulberry bush. Here we go round the mulberry bush—so early in the morning. ♫ You guessed it: the "We want water" sing-along. When the Hebrews arrived at the Desert of Zin, again there was no water.

By this time, they'd seen so many miracles it was commonplace. But similar to their previous wrongdoings, they started verbally antagonizing Moses with their other favorite song:

> *Why did you bring us up out of Egypt to die in this terrible place?! It has no grain or figs, grapevines or pomegranates. And there is no water to drink!* (Numbers 20:5).

Moses and Aaron both felt the sting of these venomous vipers and prayed to God for help. God instructed Moses to *speak* to the rock, and it would give them water. Moses, frazzled and frustrated—possibly infuriated—from all the heat he was taking, *hit* the rock instead and said a few choice words while whacking it with his staff. Water still flowed. But this was the whack that broke the camel's back. God rebuked Moses for not following His command to "speak to the rock," and as penalty, told Moses he also would not be allowed into the Promised Land.

Moses lost out on living in the land of milk and honey all because of these irritating, exasperating ingrates. Anyone responsible for such a grumbling group of ankle biters would have been provoked to punching. Not only would they have whacked the rock—they probably would have gone upside their skulls with that same staff.

These peevish people's frustrations over water, food, or Moses being in charge became thorns in Moses's and God's side. Their constant fussing and cussing over water ultimately caused Moses to miss the Promised Land. Because they never trusted and patiently waited on the Lord, they whined and moaned at every discomfort. Hearing "Why did you take us out of Egypt to die in the wilderness?" over and over finally plucked Moses's last good nerve. In Numbers 20:9, Moses snapped—calling them rebels while simultaneously thrashing the rock instead of speaking to it. He was so frustrated, he lit into the rock twice!

God bless him. It's been over 3,000 years since the Exodus, but I wish I could prostrate and intercede for Moses myself. He was provoked by those malevolent misfits. Nonetheless, God felt Moses hadn't trusted Him enough to honor Him, and therefore he wasn't allowed into the Promised Land. Moses was working with a horrible bunch of whiners. I don't know who could have survived them. I think Jesus himself would have wanted to "lay hands" on them. Poor Moses spent forty years in the wilderness for a trip that should have taken eleven days! And for all his hard work corralling these intransigent ingrates, he didn't even make it to the Promised Land!

The takeaway: if someone does something nice for you, out of kindness or necessity, say "Thank you," "That was very kind of you," or "How thoughtful." Whether you asked for it or not, simply say "thank you"—or if there's a choice to decline, kindly say "No thank you." Don't bite the hand reaching out to feed you by being a bad receiver of goodwill. A gracious giver is a blessing, but a receptive recipient also warms the heart.

Lesson number two: if your needs aren't being met, ask for what you want with a pleasant demeanor. Refrain from puckish, arrogant displays—teeth-sucking, eye-rolling, neck-twisting, lip-curling, hands-on-hips. A Real Housewives attitude is obnoxious to God and will cause delayed blessings or none at all. In all circumstances, let the Fruits of the Holy Spirit guide your demeanor: Love, Joy, Peace, Patience, Kindness, Goodness, Faithfulness, Gentleness, and Self-control. Against such things there is no law (Galatians 5:22-23).

Map 2. Exodus Escape Route Map

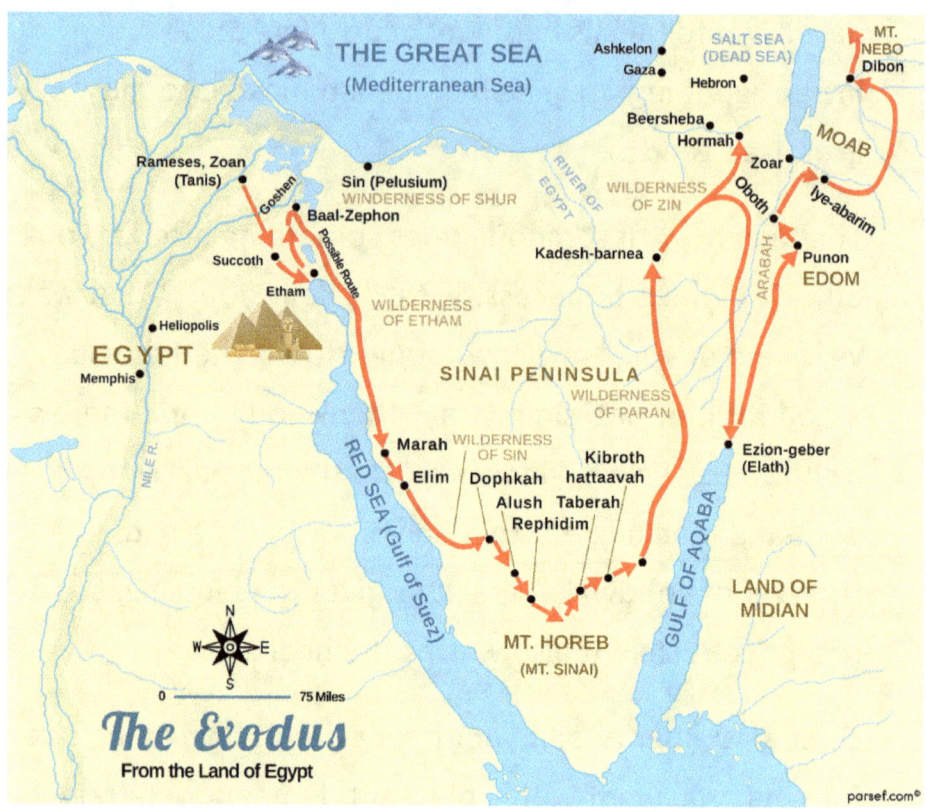

(Bible History Online, 2025)

3 JONAH'S UNWISE CHOICES WERE BAD FOR HIS HEALTH AND OTHERS

The prophet Jonah had serious issues with lack of compassion and way too much self-righteousness. At times, all humans suffer from self-righteousness— blinded by our own brilliance and failing to see our own faults. Thankfully, God used this very brief book in the Bible to show all of us how screwed up we are, thinking we're God's gift to creation.

God instructed Jonah to go to Nineveh and prophesy to the people that He would bring wrath upon them. This type of assignment wasn't unusual. God did this with Isaiah, Hosea, Jeremiah, Elijah, Elisha, Ezekiel, and many others. Remember Sodom and Gomorrah? On the way to annihilating those two sin cities, God stopped by His friend Abraham's home and had a nice lunch with him and Sarah. As He left, He told Abraham He was going to check out the wickedness He'd heard about in Sodom and Gomorrah—and if any of it was true, He would destroy everything in them. Abraham was shocked and alarmed because his nephew Lot lived in Sodom. So Abraham petitioned God over and over to spare the towns if a certain number of righteous people were found. God assured Abraham that if He found only five righteous people, He would spare the cities. God kept His word because He loves us. Even though He ultimately obliterated Sodom and Gomorrah, He saved Lot and his family. So Jonah's assignment was more of the same. God is generous, loving, and slow to anger— He sends us warnings and messengers to get our attention.

But "holier than thou" Jonah felt it was a waste of his time because the folks in Nineveh weren't going to straighten up and fly right. In his opinion. When God told Jonah, "Go to the great city of Nineveh and preach against it, because its wickedness has come up before me" (Jonah 1:1, NIV), Jonah tried to flee instead of heed. And when he decided to run away, he began to foolishly push a boulder up a steep hill.

Had Jonah obeyed, he would have made the three-day journey east from Israel to Nineveh. Instead, he boarded a ship heading west for Tarshish, Spain—3,600 miles in the opposite direction. That was only the beginning of Jonah's extremely asinine odyssey. The most obvious point he missed: you can't outrun God. He is everywhere.

The second thing I took from Jonah's misguided attempt to flee was how he put innocent lives in danger. He endangered others who had no idea they were harboring a fugitive of God. Jonah boarded a ship, and because God knew exactly where he was, He sent a violent storm that almost broke the ship to pieces. But where was Jonah during all this mayhem? Below deck, peacefully sleeping, while the people upstairs were reeling for their lives.

Doesn't that always seem to be the case? You're innocently going about your life, minding your own business, when a reckless, unwise, or downright unintelligent person comes along, brings all kinds of calamity, disrupts your life, and—wham!—you're now a casualty of someone else's poor choices. Either they've cost you money, or something even more important: your life, or the life of a loved one.

Jonah had no idea he was the cause of all the ruckus— but sadly, a fool never does. Jonah's rebelliousness caused Nothing But Trouble[10], bringing disaster to himself and anyone near him. The saddest part? He wasn't even aware. The captain woke him up and yelled, "How can you sleep? Get up and call on your God. Maybe he will notice us, and we won't die" (Jonah 1:6, GW). Not waiting for Jonah to do the right thing—because they now recognized he was less than bright—they drew straws to see who caused this nightmare. Of course, Jonah got the short straw, so they began sternly interrogating him. "Who are you?! Where did you come from?! What did you do?!"

The men already knew he was running from the Lord. When Jonah confessed it was because of him all this was happening, they became truly frightened. In some Bible translations, Jonah had previously told them (perhaps while boarding) that he was running from God. Apparently, they didn't think much of this important bit of information.

For future reference: when someone comes to you for help, please use wisdom and discernment before extending a hand. You may determine this person's life is steeped in foolishness and turmoil—confirmation they are out of God's will. If so, give them a big fat "No." Should you take in this imprudent person, not only are you setting yourself up for disaster, you're endangering those you love.

Having learned the hard way that Jonah was causing all this havoc, the sailors felt they had to try and Sail On[11] despite the violent conditions. Compassionately, they tried to take the high road and not throw Jonah to his death in the raging sea. But once they took it upon themselves to offer conveyance to God's fugitive, they bore the brunt of Jonah's recklessness. Their vessel was now attached to a giant boulder-anchor and deteriorating fast. The seas became more violent, to the point where they couldn't continue with their disagreeable cargo. So after a brief "adios amigo, bon voyage," they tossed the unwelcomed vagabond overboard. Without delay, the seas calmed and the men praised God Almighty who quiets violent seas.

As for poor, pitiful Jonah, things only got worse. This is the usual course of waywardness. Life will go from bad to worse until that light-bulb moment happens and we finally figure out all of this could have been avoided had we done the right thing from the get-go. Well, God gave Jonah plenty of time to think—inside the stinking belly of a huge fish. As fantastic as it sounds, I truly believe

God kept the fish from digesting Jonah. And while Jonah sat in the rotten stench of the fish's bowels, he had all the time in the world to figure out how he went off the rails with his harebrained plan to outrun God Almighty.

During those three days and three nights, I'm willing to bet Jonah came to the same conclusion over and over: "I should have gone to Nineveh." He probably cursed his every action from the moment he decided to flee to Tarshish. He probably gave himself a loud Sanford and Son[12] scolding: "You big dummy!" No one could hear him—why not let out all his self-inflicted castigations? The smartest thing Jonah did while in that smelly fish was pray out to God in praise and ask for deliverance.

Jonah's light-bulb moment had finally come. He realized he needed God to be merciful and lenient on him—the same way God wanted to give leniency and forbearance to those people in Nineveh. Jonah wanted desperately for God not to leave him where he was, not to cast him out of His sight. Jonah repented—albeit after much encouragement from his present situation—but nonetheless, he repented. That's all God wanted from Nineveh: for them to repent and come to their senses before things got really ugly.

Had Jonah done what was smart and right from the start, things wouldn't have gotten ugly and smelly for him. But before things could get completely better, Jonah had to be vomited out of the fish. I imagine it was far worse and way messier leaving the fish than going in.

Once out and back on dry land, God again commanded Jonah to go to Nineveh. And once he got there, he did what the Lord commanded and prophesied throughout the city: "Forty days more and Nineveh will be overthrown!" (Jonah 3:3). And you know what? The people actually did the right thing and quickly repented. They respected the Lord so much, they put on sackcloth, sat in dust, and fasted. Everyone from the least to the greatest sincerely repented because they feared and believed God. The king of Nineveh even made a formal decree that everyone should fast and repent so God would forgive them. And when God saw all of this, His anger was quelled. He had compassion and mercy on them and did not carry out His plan to destroy them.

God's compassion toward Nineveh angered Jonah. He childishly fumed that he knew from the beginning God would relent and not do anything to those people—and that was why he didn't want to do this mission in the first place. What a forgetful, arrogant idiot. Didn't he receive the same type of pardon from our great compassionate and forgiving God? So why was he taking umbrage at God giving others the same kindness, as if they didn't deserve the same grace?

Jonah became so colossally ticked off, he marched out of the city like a pouty-faced child and figuratively poked out his bottom lip. In inexplicable anger, he sat on the ground under a shelter and watched repugnantly to see what would happen to Nineveh. I believe God probably found Jonah's theatrics comical as well as pitiful, which is why He didn't wring his stiff little neck and put him in his place.

Being merciful and trying to get Jonah to see the big picture, God allowed a plant to grow up overnight to protect him from the scorching sun. This shady plant made Jonah very happy. However, the next day it died because a worm attacked it. That same day, God sent an east wind and let the sun beat down on Jonah's bare head. Jonah passed out from the intense heat! When he came to, he became even more upset because his plant died—and impetuously wished he would die. Poor, silly

Jonah was mad at the wrong person for all the wrong reasons.

God asked Jonah why he was angry about a plant dying that he had no part in giving life to in the first place. And why was he more compassionate about a plant but angry at God for showing kindness to 120,000 innocent human beings and all the blameless animals that would have been destroyed? Sadly, Jonah remained hopelessly indifferent toward the people of Nineveh. The lesson of compassion was lost on him.

Jonah's earlier foolishness nearly cost several people their lives, and God forgave him. Yet he sat foolishly sulking outside in the sweltering heat, angrily wishing to die because God refused to snuff out remorseful people.

What a powerful yet humorous lesson God provided us on humanity and compassion through the prophet Jonah. The other great lessons gleaned from Jonah's life:

(1) You can't reach everyone. (2) Jonah brought all this on himself when he willfully decided not to follow and obey God. (3) If possible, avoid unnecessary entanglements with unwise people. Help them from a distance, but do not endanger your life, your livelihood,

or the lives of your loved ones for a risky, illogical, and unreachable person. Peril follows them like a moth to a flame. And lastly, (4) If you recognize yourself in Jonah or your life is a Lemony Snicket's A Series of Unfortunate Events[13], sit down someplace quiet and read the book of Proverbs. It's an essential starting point for acquiring wisdom and discernment to eventually reduce and remove misfortune plaguing your life. The teachings in Proverbs are priceless, life-changing, and life-saving.

Map 3. Map of Jonah's Idiotic Odyssy

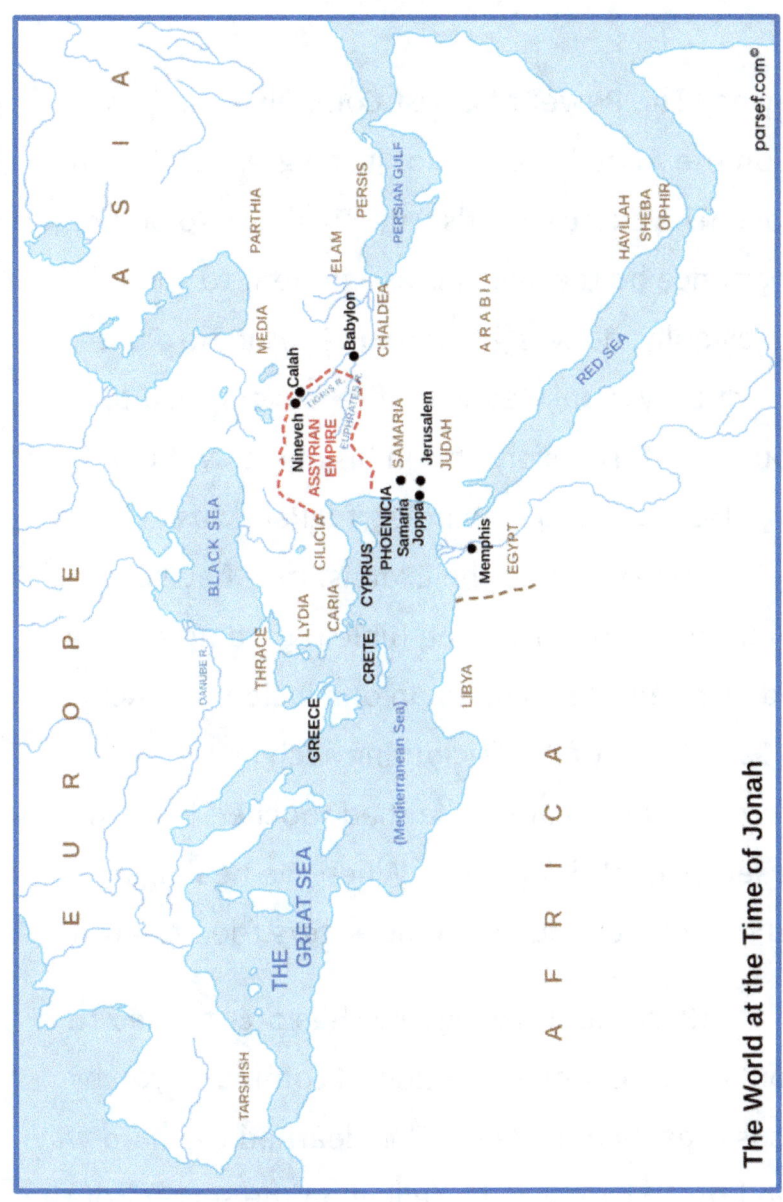

The World at the Time of Jonah

(Bible History Online, 2025)

4 PAUL, VICARIOUS DEMON SLAYER AND DEADLY ORATOR

The saying "The Power of Christ Compels You..." was based on the Apostle Paul—not just a great tagline in the movie The Exorcist[14]. It's true. Paul was so on fire for God that once he received his assignment to spread the gospel, by golly, he was going to do it! And he did it enthusiastically! Paul was so on fire, others tried to vicariously perform exorcisms in his name. Not only was it a huge testament to how powerful Paul was in Jesus's name—it further proves The Exorcist may have been loosely based on details in the Bible regarding all Paul did and inspired others to do. In one incident in Acts 19:11-12, articles of Paul's clothing such as handkerchiefs and scarves that had touched his skin were used to heal sick people. When the healings proved to work, of course the hucksters tried to profit.

In Acts 19:13, some traveling Jewish exorcists tried to drive out demons while shouting, "I command you by the Jesus preached by Paul." They learned the hard way you can't do an exorcism by calling on the servant of the Master. You need to call on the Master Himself. The demon spirit said, "Jesus I know, and Paul I've heard of. But who are you?" Not only were these bootleg exorcists unqualified—they were pathetically unsuccessful. The undeterred demon went totally berserk, turned around, and beat the daylights out of them, leaving them naked, bleeding, battered, bruised, and running for their lives.

That was a cautionary example of why not to perform exorcisms willy-nilly. I'm not saying you need special skills or training per se, but you will need confidence, conviction, and bass in your voice on the level of Barry White.

In Acts 16:16, Paul and Silas's nonstop walking, traveling, and evangelizing absolutely fatigued them. This exhaustion created in Paul a zero tolerance for nonsense or annoying people. On one particularly fateful occasion, his irritability led him to lose his temper on a demon-possessed slave girl who would not stop praising him and Silas. She followed them everywhere, constantly saying, "These men are the servants of the Most High God, who proclaim to us the way of salvation." After a few days, this girl's excessive exaltations got up underneath Paul's nerves. While metamorphosing into the Incredible Hulk[15], all manner of unrestrained grouchiness spewed out of Paul's twisted face, and in guttural tones he ordered, "I command you in the name of Jesus Christ to come out of her. And he came out that very hour" (Acts 16:18).

Paul's aggressive attitude was deserved. Nobody has time to mince words when driving out demons. Irrespective of the fact that the demon spoke favorably about them, it makes no difference. Demons are Bad News Bears[16] and should be violently exterminated without dilly-dallying. Unfortunately, Paul and Silas were jailed and beaten for this incident because this huckster's hustle was All About the Benjamins[17]. Acts 16:19 explains: "When her masters saw that their hope of profit was gone, they seized Paul and Silas and dragged them into the marketplace to the authorities."

Paul's resurrection power worked because he was commanding and confident when he spoke to demons. He stood on the affirming truth of Jesus Christ. The others were counterfeits who either didn't believe in the power of Christ or were merely doing it for profit. Confirmation of what Jesus spoke in Matthew 7:16: "You will know them by their fruits."

Due to Paul's demon-slayer chronicles and the fact that people of varying beliefs also tried doing it in his name, Paul came to be highly esteemed, propelling the Gospel of Jesus Christ all over the province of Ephesus. Many professed witches and warlocks burned their sorcery books to lay aside all that was contrary to the Way of Jesus Christ because of Paul's supernatural repute.

Unfortunately, this charlatan's prophetess was all geared toward profit. It didn't matter that she was saying good things about Paul and Silas. On that auspicious day, she was the notorious thorn in Paul's side, and he righteously knocked the devil out of her with the Word.

Not only was Paul a dynamite demon slayer, he was most renowned for his eloquent letters in the Bible. But on the flip side, he was also a notoriously incessant talker. Yep, you heard right. He was a "chatterbox," "motormouth," "chatty-Cathy," "gum-flapper"—aka "Sir Talks-a-Lot." This next story may be one of the most hilarious examples of what not to do at your next dinner party.

We all know people who can talk a Blue Streak[18] and only need an occasional "uh huh" or head nod.

Sometimes these incessant windbags don't even need that. They only need the whites of your eyes and they'll blab on for hours without pause or allowing you a much-needed bathroom break. Once they lock eyes on you, out of politeness, you feel bound to give them your attention. These "talk-aholics" are unconcerned that you're entering in and out of consciousness or literally looking for the nearest escape hatch.

What about people who seem to have held in their words all day? When they finally catch an unsuspecting victim—I mean listener—they exhale every pent-up word without taking a breath. You feel like your hair is standing up as if you've been through a wind tunnel. At social gatherings, others look upon the captured prey with pity, thinking, "That poor fellow" or "That poor gal." What they don't do is step in and take the chatterbox off your hands. I know this to be true because I've fallen victim on many occasions. And I've witnessed others tortured into comas until their eyes twitched, or talked to the point of a splitting headache, without so much as someone asking a fake question to take the boiling pot off the burner.

Boy! It'd be great if we could spew out a truth tirade like Steve Martin did to blabbermouth John Candy in the motel room scene in Planes Trains and Automobiles[19]. Alas, most folks are afraid to interrupt an oblivious, longwinded lecturer. Perhaps this is the price we pay to live in a civilized society. The sufferers would be considered rude to tell the gabbers to put a sock in it. The tragic irony is that the victims are labeled rude or boorish and potentially never invited to another party. But what about the person who doesn't know how to behave in a chit-chat? You chit, they chat. It's a back-and-forth exchange of brief pleasantries. If it evolves into more significant topics, it should be mutually agreed upon, as evinced by increased liveliness of the exchanges. Once either party shows boredom, distress, or uncontrolled eye twitching, one should promptly abort! If the cloddish person does not stop, in my humble opinion, they are uncouth and could use a refresher from Miss Manners.

I believe Paul was truly anointed by the Holy Spirit. God put an unquenchable fire inside of Paul which compelled him to preach the Word with passion, zeal, and conviction—and regrettably, without a stop button.

In Acts 20, Paul and other traveling apostles were at a stopover in Troas, Asia (modern-day Turkey). The men agreed to meet in the upper room of the local congregation and have Sunday dinner. The plan: eat dinner, chill out, and leave early the next morning. Then Paul started talking. One story led to another, which led to another. Paul could preach the gospel like nobody's business. Before long, it was past midnight.

A young man named Eutychus happened to take the seat at the open window. As Paul talked, he failed to recognize the warning signs to abort. Eutychus was fading fast and heading for a 911[20] emergency. But Paul would not shut up. The next thing they heard was Eutychus hitting the outside stoop three stories below. He had lapsed into a coma during Paul's nonstop talking and fallen out the window. Out cold, Eutychus didn't even scream while falling. When they went down and picked him up, Eutychus was dead!

Not to worry. Being full of God's resurrection power, Paul stretched himself over the poor guy and bear-hugged him. He brought the boy back to life without a glitch. Then Paul confidently exclaimed, "Don't be alarmed! He is alive, all is well!" Did windbag Paul just gloss over the trivial fact that he killed Eutychus?

After his triumphant update regarding Eutychus's medical status, Paul went back upstairs, served the much-delayed Sunday dinner, then resumed talking until dawn! After all that talking, no one had even eaten! No wonder Eutychus passed out—he was famished to the point of a migraine. Didn't Paul see the boy's eye twitching and the pulsating vein along his forehead? If ever there was a need for a gum-flapper's intervention, it was at that dinner party.

The lesson: talk responsibly. If not for Paul's incessant talking, Eutychus would neither have fallen, died, nor required CPR. But if you're going to be a chatterbox, have the resurrection, Holy-Ghost power like Paul—or a portable defibrillator. An unsuspecting victim may need emergency life-saving measures should they face-plant out of a high window because of a rude chatterbox.

Map 4. Eutychus's Fall & Map of Paul's Visit

Source: https://missionbibleclass.org/1b0-new-testament/new-testament-part-2/acts-epistle-selections/eutychus-falls-from-a-window/ Accessed: 3/30/2018

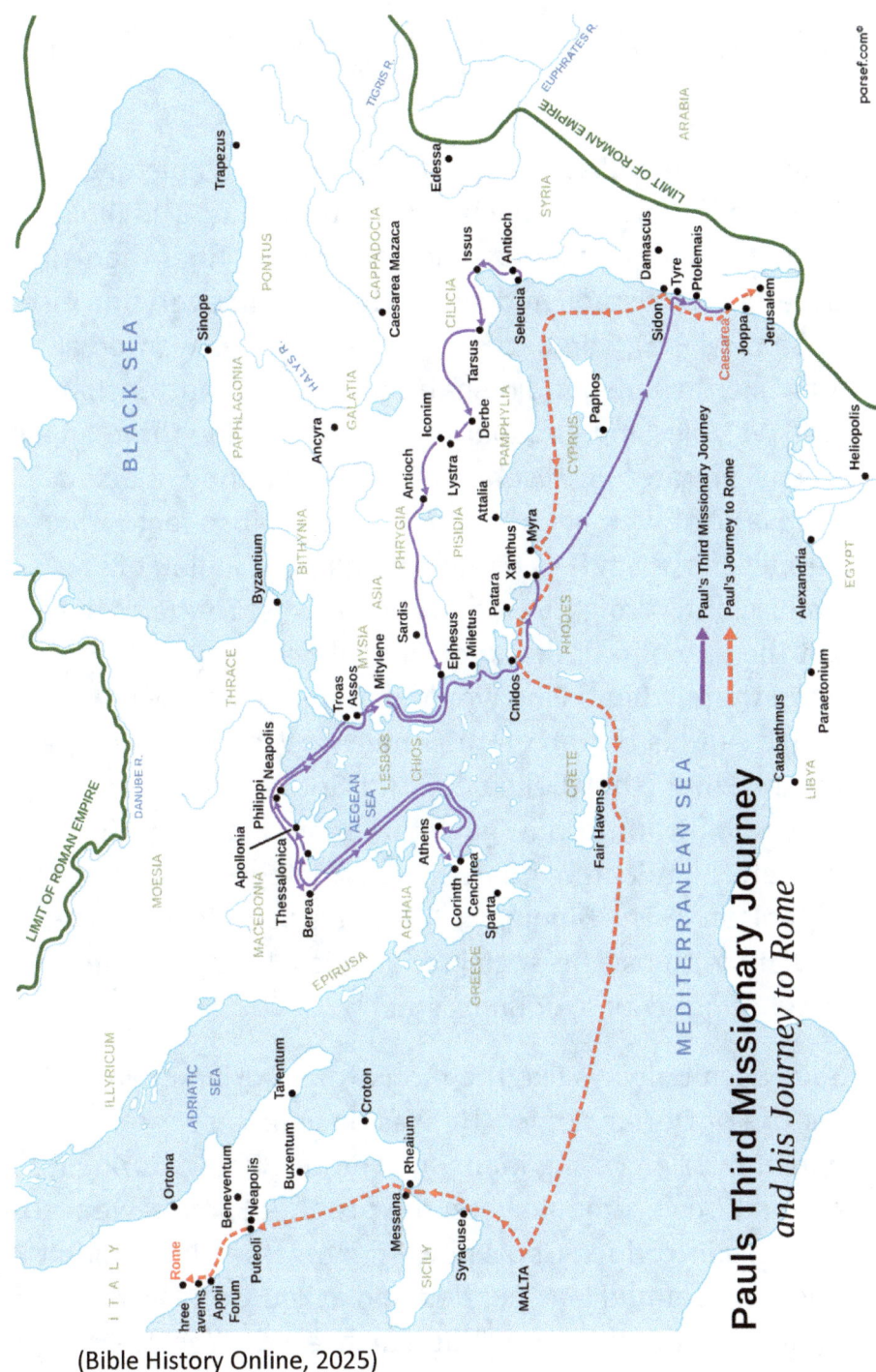

Pauls Third Missionary Journey
and his Journey to Rome

(Bible History Online, 2025)

5 SAUL, THE MANY FACES OF CRAY-CRAY

When I think of Saul, the first king of Israel, I picture a jock. An "all bronze, tiny brains" type of guy. The Bible describes him as a handsome young man, finer than all other men in Israel, and a head taller than everyone else (1 Samuel 9:2). The backstory: the Israelites wanted a king like the surrounding nations. It didn't matter that God was blessing, prospering, and defending them on all sides. Ungratefully disobedient as usual, they rejected Jehovah Yahweh and demanded a king. Ipso facto, the people chose Saul—a handsome half-wit in lieu of omniscient, Almighty God. Unbeknownst to them, they got the raw end of that foolish deal. Samuel tried to warn them what a king would demand and how he would put his thumb on their necks. "We don't care! We want a king!" they bellowed. And God, all-wise and exceedingly humorous, gave them the desires of their ungrateful, rejecting hearts: Saul. Analogous to Jack Nicholson in The Shining[21], "Heeere's Saul! Pretty-faced deviant with psycho-social tendencies. Enjoy your new rabid-minded king, you ingrates!"

Saul wasn't always like the monstrous Dorian in The Picture of Dorian Gray[22]. He was once an insecure, shy, and endearing young man. In 1 Samuel 10:21, during his coronation ceremony when the prophet Samuel went to officially introduce God's new King of Israel, he couldn't find him. Samuel was puzzled and asked God, "Is the man you anointed here?" God answered, "Yes, He is hiding among the supplies." Ridiculously, Saul was hiding among the supplies like a slapstick comedian. In the same vein as Jerry Lewis, Carol Burnett, or John Ritter, I chuckle at the thought of silly Saul hiding in plain sight between mops, brooms, and buckets, with stringy mop locks covering his face. So terrified of his new position, he desperately tried to be invisible.

To be fair, it's not unusual to be nervous when you're not accustomed to the limelight. Saul was young and unknown—more than likely chosen because he fit the protesters' biases of what a king should look like. Proof[23] of this assessment is in 1 Samuel 16. Because Saul refused to obey God, Samuel was ordered to anoint a new king. After seeing one of David's brothers, Samuel thought, he must be the chosen one. And God said, "Do not consider his appearance or his height, for I have rejected him. The Lord does not look at the things people look at. People look at the outward appearance, but the Lord looks at the heart" (1 Samuel 16:7). This tells me the people were impressed with Saul's good looks. Regardless, he was incompetent. Saul knew without a doubt he was unqualified. But once anointed, I don't think a polite "Thank you so much, but no thanks" was acceptable. It may not have been an option. One thing is certain: Saul's meteoric rise to fame was evidently too overwhelming even for him. In the harmless hiding In Plain Sight[24] scenario, Saul was insecure but not a raging loon. However, stay tuned. His inner demons will let loose on the belligerent "boo-hooers" soon enough!

The famous quote, "I've seen firsthand that being president doesn't change who you are. It reveals who you are" (Obama, n.d.), is true of monarchs, czars, and world leaders too. Saul's senselessness and cruelty were brought to full-on display soon after he became king. The person inside him was not merely an insecure people-pleaser. He was a foul-mouthed, self-serving, demented, paranoid-schizophrenic. At first glance, you may have missed all these unholy characteristics. So I will carefully pull back the drapes on this afflicted screwball. To put a period on his previously mentioned malady of insecurity and people-pleasing, carefully meditate on this: At that same coronation event, once the ceremony was over, Saul overheard some men viciously dissing him. They brought him no gifts and audibly questioned how Saul could save them, as if to say he was a big loser! Saul overheard everything and chose to say not a word. He was the king and they were his subjects. He could have had those treasonous traitors punished or killed. But he chose to be liked, so kept silent.

Regarding Saul's frenzied or demented state, two incidents come to mind. The first was his very first act as new king. Nahash, the Ammonite king, and his troops surrounded the Israelite town of Jabesh Gilead and told them to surrender or else. The elders said okay, but first let us send word to our brethren, and if no one responds we'll give ourselves up. What a civil and polite way to besiege a territory. A very gentlemanly warfare indeed. No rancorous display of valor. No threats to push big red buttons. Rather a polite, "Cheerio, we've come to invade you, now give up or else," met with an equally polite, "Sure thing. But first allow me to make a few calls for help, and I'll give you my answer shortly." English accent and all.

When word got back to Saul regarding his subjects' precarious situation, it says the Spirit of the Lord came powerfully upon him. Saul was fired up! That was good, right? Well, it would have been had he simply gone up and rescued his people. Instead, to inspire them, using a Hacksaw[25], he hewed two oxen into pieces and had them couriered throughout the land. The purpose of his insane mass mailing campaign was to depict what would happen to anyone's cattle if they did not follow Saul and Samuel in battling the enemy. Imagine the terror after opening that blood-soaked package. It was truly horrifying and did spark terror. The Bible said, "Then the terror of the Lord fell on the people and they came out together as one" (1 Samuel 11:7). No one should be surprised the people came out as commanded. The purpose and method to his madness achieved his desired response. God bless him, I suppose. If the Lord be with him, who can be against him? But wow! Really Saul? That seems a bit shocking, I'm just saying.

Let's assume his first act of crazy was a fluke. And it was necessary for him to slice and dice the livestock and letter-bomb their body parts to his people. How else would they know he was serious? Okay, we'll let that incident slide. But check out Saul's second scenario of "Crazy As A Soup Sandwich"[26] shenanigans.

During a heated battle between Saul's army and the hated Philistines, Saul decreed none of his men could eat anything until evening, or before he avenged himself on his enemies (see 1 Samuel 14:24). This was a foolish and stupid rule, especially for fighting men. They needed their strength to fight, for heaven's sake. Who in their right mind would restrict a soldier from food, knowing huge amounts of calories are expended during guerilla warfare? Someone who is not mentally sound. Saul's son Jonathan happened to not hear his father's proclamation and ate some energizing honey while hiding out in the woods. The other troops informed him of his blunder. Even Jonathan knew it was stupid; keeping fighting men faint and dizzy with hunger is absolutely not military intelligence.

Later that day when the men finally defeated the enemy, like white on rice they pounced on the pillaged animals and butchered them with their bare hands. The soldiers were so famished and out of control, they started eating the freshly bludgeoned and bleeding beasts. Silly Saul had the audacity to tell the men they had broken faith because of their sin of eating meat with the lifeblood still in it. He was the "idgit galoot" who put them in that untenable situation. What did he think would happen? Polite chit-chat over hors d'oeuvres and an orderly, neatly snaked buffet line? No! At this point, the men were darn near cannibalistic. Luckily those animals were there, otherwise they might have eaten one another like those stranded people in the movie Alive[27].

If not for the courage of the other soldiers who took up for and rescued Jonathan, he would have been killed at the hands of his madcap father. After insanely ordering his men not to eat, Saul decided to punish his own son with death for disobeying his thoughtless order. This would not be the only time Saul would lash out cruelly at his own son. Time after time, without provocation or reason, Saul murderously lashed out at his loyal and most undeserving subjects.

Not too long after Saul was made king, as we've already witnessed, cracks in his sanity started to manifest. Once God removed His anointing on Saul and placed it on David, Saul's mental deterioration accelerated. Serendipitously, Saul's mania was the impetus behind one of the greatest bromances in human history, spurring David and Jonathan to become closer than brothers.

In 1 Samuel 18:11, Saul asked David to play the lyre to help soothe his savage mood swings. In a sudden fit of rage, he hurled a spear at David, trying to pin him to the wall. I guess in Saul's twisted mind, assassination was how he showed appreciation. And to show his son Jonathan affection, he cannon-blasted him with verbal obscenities as if he was a stray dog. Yep, Saul was "good ole" Mommy Dearest[28] and not at all Father Knows Best[29]. Take a look at how he sweetly talks about his own son and wife.

When David reported to his best friend Jonathan that Saul was trying to kill him, Jonathan tried to give his father the benefit of the doubt. But Jonathan didn't dismiss his friend's feelings by saying, "You're crazy man! My father wouldn't do that!" No, Jonathan put David's mind at ease and told him he would get to the bottom of David's concerns and let him know what he found out regarding Saul's true inclinations.

During the New Moon feast, Jonathan and David devised a plan to find out exactly where Saul's mind was. They agreed David would purposely be absent from the feast at Saul's palace both days of the celebration. The first night at dinner, Saul noticed David was absent but assumed he must have been ritually unclean and couldn't partake in the feast. All seemed okay. No big whoop. The next day, however, Saul noticed David was absent again and asked Jonathan, "Why hasn't the son of Jesse come to the meal, either yesterday or today?" Jonathan told his father, David had asked to go to his own home for religious reasons and he had given him his blessing.

Without counting to ten or taking a deep breath, Saul screamed, "You son of a perverse and rebellious woman!" Translation: "You son of a slut!" Either way, Saul called his son Jonathan "a son of a whore" (see 1 Samuel 20:1-30). I envision Jonathan lunging at Saul, yelling, "Now wait a minute, you crazy old man! Don't you call my mother a whore!?" It probably took every cupbearer, dishwasher, and groundskeeper on duty to keep Jonathan from swinging on his out-to-lunch father. Only a crazed lunatic would verbally attack his son and wife with thoughtless, venomous, and injurious insults.

Would Saul sink any deeper into cray-cray? Yes, the depths of which one can't begin to imagine.

For an example of his paranoid-schizophrenia, let's explore Saul's next out-of-his-mind episode. And again, this was all because Saul was jealous of David. To get away from the deranged madman, David fled to the town of Nob. There, he went to the sanctuary and asked Ahimelek the priest if he had any bread to eat and weapons for fighting. He may have told the man of God an "alternative fact" when he said he and his men were on a last-minute secret mission for King Saul. The priest had no reason to disbelieve David—he was one of Saul's most loyal soldiers and a decorated war hero who had defeated Goliath. Without a second thought, the priest gave him the old consecrated bread and the sword that belonged to Goliath. Then he bid him an innocent farewell (see 1 Samuel 21:1-9).

Unfortunately, a "snake-in-the-grass" named Doeg the Edomite was at the sanctuary when David was there. Doeg was Saul's chief shepherd, and he overheard everything! Sure enough, he told Saul all he observed. As innocuous as Ahimelek's actions were, paranoid Saul was convinced in his precarious mental state that the priest was in collusion with David and conspired against his throne. Not only did Saul accuse God's anointed priest of seditious acts, he diabolically ordered his men to kill Ahimelek and all his family. Saul's soldiers refused to raise a hand against God's priest. Saul then commanded obsequious Doeg the Edomite to do it, who happily obliged. Without the sense of a goose, Saul foolishly wiped out a whole line of godly men, 85 in all (1 Samuel 22:16-19). Each unyielding, homicidal, Livin' La Vida Loca[30] meltdown dug Saul's grave deeper and deeper. I could be wrong, but murdering God's consecrated and holy priests is a bad thing. Why else would his soldiers disobey a direct order? Their refusal didn't faze mad King Saul one bit. He was too far gone for any sound reasoning.

Saul's brain had taken a flying leap. Much like the leap the character "Chief" took out that broken window in One Flew Over the Cuckoo's Nest[31]. And remember, David playing the lyre was Saul's only relief. At this juncture, I doubt David ever played soothing music for Saul again. Perhaps at his funeral, but not while he was alive. Umm, no thank you! Like the slobbering, rabid, bat-bitten hound in Cujo[32], Saul's mood swings were erratic and unpredictable. You never knew when he would attack. And the sad part: David never had any issues with Saul. But Saul hunted David for sport—all because of his irrational jealousy.

A valuable lesson for anyone plagued with sudden inexplicable spells of absurdity and lack of self control: There might be areas of disobedience and unchecked jealousy requiring your immediate attention. It's neither demure nor endearing to be a jealous, delusional, murderous, pathological predator. Without a doubt, God will blot you out.

6 BALAAM OR THE DONKEY, WHICH ONE IS THE JACKASS?

Not to beat a dead horse, but let me remind you about the Hebrews' 40-year journey through the wilderness covered in chapter two. Don't worry though. This story is not focused on them right now. But at the very end of this tale, I will provide a juicy update. Trust me! You will want to hear how they got themselves into deep doo-doo for reasons similar to why creepin' Craig got fired in the movie Friday[33]. For now, let's begin with Balaam and his donkey.

While the Israelites were sojourning in the wilderness, they looked like a great hoard to all the nations witnessing their migration. Naturally, they put fear into the hearts of the surrounding nations. Especially fearful were the Moabites, who had been freshly conquered by the Amorites, hence their edginess. Not only was their land stolen, their sons and daughters became fugitives and captives of Sihon, King of the Amorites (Numbers 21:29). When the Moabites saw the Israelites and all their many fighting men, they were frightened into a frenzy. They said, "This horde is going to lick up everything around us as an ox licks up the grass of the field" (Numbers 22, NIV).

The Israelites, however, were not looking for a fight or to cause trouble. Had the Moabites understood what was happening, they would have appreciated how Almighty God was destroying all the wicked Canaanite descendants, including the enemy Amorites. This was the purpose of the Hebrews leaving Egypt. Not only to be freed from Pharaoh—God was also systematically exterminating the Canaanites and giving the land to the Israelites. Faithfully keeping His promise made to Abraham, then to Isaac, and then to Jacob centuries prior. Out of fear, Balak the Moabite king decided to call on a sorcerer to curse the Hebrews so he could defeat them.

Balak summoned Balaam from the area of Pethor to come to Moab and put a curse on the Israelites. He said the people were too powerful for him and wanted Balaam to curse them because whomever Balaam cursed was cursed, and whomever Balaam blessed was blessed. They put a lot of faith in Balaam and promised him a ton of money. Balaam was a sorcerer for hire; a pay-to-play prophet, or in this case a pay-to-pray prophet. He was willing to do whatever was asked, as long as the money was in his hand at the end of the transaction. But God had the final say in this deal with a devil.

God told Balaam He did not want him to go anywhere with Moab's representatives. However, Balaam's greed would not allow him to be obedient. He truly did not want to send the Moabite financiers away without collecting what they were offering. So Balaam stalled them and said he would inquire of the Lord and find out what he could do for them. God already told Balaam, "Do not go with them. You must not put a curse on those people because they are blessed" (Numbers 22).

But Balaam was determined to get what he wanted out of this unholy transaction. When Balaam inquired of God a second time, God told him he could go with them if the emissary came back. That was all Balaam needed to hear. Without hesitating or meditating on God's instructions, he saddled his donkey and left with the envoy. Which was what he wanted to do all along.

Because Balaam was hell-bent on taking this profit-driven trip to Moab, an angel of the Lord stood on the road to oppose him. Defiant Balaam was now under God's wrath for going his own way. Fortunately, Balaam's donkey was able to see the angel of the Lord, but Balaam could not. When the donkey saw the angel with His sword drawn, he veered off the road into a field. Frustrated and impatient at the donkey for keeping him from his pay, Balaam beat the donkey back onto the road. The angel of the Lord appeared to Balaam's donkey a second time. This time it was on a very narrow path through a vineyard. The donkey was so spooked, it pressed very close to the wall and crushed Balaam's foot. So Balaam beat the donkey again. Then the angel of the Lord appeared to the donkey for a third time, and now there was no room to move left or right, so the donkey just sat down under Balaam. That was it for Balaam. The donkey had made a fool out of him three times, so he beat his donkey like a piñata with his staff.

Then God opened the donkey's mouth, and it said to Balaam, "What have I done to you to make you beat me these three times?" Balaam answered the donkey, "You have made a fool of me! If only I had a sword in my hand

I would kill you right now." The donkey said to Balaam, "Am I not your own donkey, which you have always ridden to this day? Have I been in the habit of doing this to you?" "No," he said (Numbers 22:29-30, NIV). After this back and forth between Balaam and his donkey, the Lord finally opened Balaam's blind eyes, and he saw what the donkey had already seen. Standing on the road in front of him was the angel of the Lord wielding His sword.

The donkey was smarter than Balaam because it saw the danger in front of them. The angel of the Lord said, "Why have you beaten your donkey these three times? I have come here to oppose you because your path is a reckless one before me. The donkey saw me and turned away these three times. If it had not turned away, I would certainly have killed you by now, but I would have spared it" (Numbers 22:32-33, NIV).

Balaam finally realized he was as wrong as two left shoes. Not only was he out of line for beating the brakes off his donkey, he was dead wrong for heading down this reckless path in pursuit of ill-gotten gain. God already told Balaam the Israelites were blessed by Him and told him not to curse them. What part of that did he not understand? God meant what He said. Because Balaam insisted on his endeavor to obtain a windfall from his Moabite benefactors, he made God very angry. When God tells you not to do something, don't try to circumvent His instructions with your own moronic methods. This is called "works of the flesh" and will in all likelihood turn out much like Balaam's jackass scenario.

Replete with frustrations and countless setbacks, you'll end up looking like a fool for not having the sense of a donkey.

And look how faithful God was to the Israelites as He continued to work all things out for their good. When rapacious Balaam arrived in Moab, God forced his mouth-for-hire to speak repeated blessings over the Israelites, on every hill in Moab, despite the fact that Moab wanted Balaam to curse them. And what were the Israelites doing? They were back at Shittim behaving shiftily. Assuming God was distracted and wouldn't find out, the men started engaging in immorality with the Moabite women who invited them to sex ceremonies for their deities. Isn't that a punch in the gut? God was forcing blessings out of the mouth of their enemy, and these blockheads repaid Him in the most disgusting and unholy way. The Moabites did sexually perverted acts in worship of their gods, and Israel knew better.

Can you guess how God dealt with these unfaithful miscreants? You guessed right. God unleashed another deadly plague on everyone partaking in the scandalous acts with the seductive Moabite women. The deadly outbreak stopped only after Phinehas, son of Eleazar, grandson of Aaron the priest, zealously put to the sword one of the immoral Israelite men who brazenly fornicated with a Moabite woman right in front of Moses and the other Israelite elders. God's anger was mollified because He saw how much Phinehas loved Him when he slayed the man and that tacky tart who dared to disrespect God Most High.

Lesson learned here: when God is silent, it doesn't mean He is gone or doesn't see what's going on. He is busy working things out and ordering your steps. And while He's quietly working, remain calm, faithful, and obedient so you can enjoy all those blessings once they manifest. It's tough to enjoy blessings when you've been zapped by God for behaving unholy, unfaithfully, and disobediently.

7 PLEASE GO HOME URIAH AND SLEEP WITH YOUR WIFE!

During the reign of King David, it was common for kings to go off to war during the springtime. Well, King David was in a funk and didn't feel like going to war. Instead, he sent his right-hand man and nephew Joab to be the commander over his deployed troops. Proverbs 16:27 tells us idle hands are the devil's workshop; idle lips are his mouthpiece. This proverb could not have been truer, especially considering all the free time on David's idle hands. His laziness or funk was giving him gobs of free time that would land him in the smelting workshop belonging to Satan himself.

David awoke one evening, and perhaps like a lazy lion, yawned widely, did an overhead stretch, and gave himself a good scratch everywhere. Sleeping till dusk tends to make your joints a bit stiff and your skin itchy and dry. He then headed out to his rooftop terrace for some refreshing evening air. Lo and behold, his eyes took in the most erotically pleasing sight of a beautiful nude woman taking a bath. Blood rushed out from his brain and flooded his lower extremities. David's brain was diminished to that of an ostrich. And like a dumb ostrich, David now had less mental acuity than an adolescent boy watching the first five minutes of Barbarella[34] or watching Princess Leia wearing the golden bikini in Star Wars[35]. An idle male under the influence of powerful hormones is akin to playing with matches in the presence of jet fuel. The out-of-control fire would be consuming, and innocent people would burn.

David swiftly sent his servants to find out who this babe was. He learned she was Bathsheba; the daughter of Eliam, and the wife of Uriah; one of his fighting men. I guess he needed to know her vital statistics so he would know what to call her in the heat of lovemaking. Because he certainly didn't use Bathsheba's personally identifiable information to make an informed decision not to sleep with her. He now knew she was the wife of one of his loyal soldiers, for Pete's sake. If anything, that should have given him reason to halt. Yet he continued to have a Love Jones[36] lust for her; beckoned for her; and slept with her without being moved by any of those learned facts. David feeding his fleshly desires was paramount to Uriah's family or wellbeing.

How did God's anointed fall so far from grace? That's easy to understand. Women were David's area of weakness. All humans have areas of weakness, and women happened to be David's. This same weakness was the Achilles' heel of his son Solomon too. David didn't address his weakness and neither did his son. All humans should know and acknowledge their area(s) of weakness so they can successfully manage it—and it not manage them. Otherwise, you will be beat by whatever it is, over and over. This is not to excuse David's crude behavior, because it gets so much worse.

David and Bathsheba slept together, and right after, scripture says she went home. No mention of promises to see each other again, or even post-coitus cuddling. Talk about the walk of shame. All her nosey neighbors were out and about, feeding their goats and chickens, and here comes Bathsheba with her bed head, slinking away from the king's palace. Oh, the disgrace of it all. Bathsheba's husband was off fighting in the war and she was carrying on with the king. The worst part: Bathsheba got pregnant after their first indiscretion.

When Bathsheba told David she was pregnant, David devised a wicked scheme to cover up his sin. He sent for Uriah to come home from the war so that Uriah would sleep with his beautiful and "faithful" wife. But Uriah was too dutiful, too naïve, and too thick to do what David desperately wanted him to do.

After feigning interest in how things were going with the soldiers, adulterous David, lacking all couth or finesse, got right to the point with Uriah and said, "Go down to your house and wash your feet" (2 Samuel 11:8). In other words, go get some from your wife.

Not one to argue with his commander-in-chief, Uriah did leave David's palace. And to make sure Uriah and Bathsheba had a very lovely evening, David sent a gift basket of assorted meats. Boy, David took care of every detail down to the milieu meats. What could go wrong? Well, Uriah only got as far as David's portico and slept there all night with the rest of the servants. David was told that Uriah did not go home, and he asked him why. Reliable Uriah said, "How could I go to my house to eat and drink and make love to my wife? As surely as you live, I will not do such a thing!" (2 Samuel 11:11).

Uriah was a devoted soldier to the core. How would David ever get him to have relations with his wife? David decided to get Uriah drunk, hoping in his intoxicated state Uriah would indulge in primal and lustful activities without consideration. But even this stunt did not work. Dutiful Uriah slept outside with the servants as he had done the other nights. David could not get this man to sleep with his wife for anything. It was now time for plan B.

David wrote a letter to Joab and sent it back with Uriah. He ordered Joab to put Uriah on the front lines when they were in the heat of battle. David somehow justified this as A Perfect Murder[37], on account of he was fresh out of other Sinister[38] strategies. If Bathsheba had another man's baby that turned out to be the king's, Uriah would have every reason to bring charges against the king or even try to kill him. So David reasoned he had no choice but to kill him. David was always one to inquire of God, but in this situation, he never once called on God. Instead, he was in full-blown works of the flesh. Sure enough, Uriah was killed in battle and David's secret was safe. David, the unchecked and all-powerful king, was able to use his power and authority to take a man's wife as his own, then kill that man because who would oppose him?

Almighty God opposed him. God saw every abominable act that David did with Bathsheba and the unholy cover-up afterwards. And He was not happy. God sent Nathan the prophet to give David a dire warning in the form of a parable:

> There were two men in a certain town, one rich and the other poor. The rich man had a very large number of sheep and cattle, but the poor man had nothing except one little ewe lamb he had bought. He raised it, and it grew up with him and his children. It shared his food, drank from his cup and even slept in his arms. It was like a daughter to him.
>
> Now a traveler came to the rich man, but the rich man refrained from taking one of his own sheep or cattle to prepare a meal for the traveler who had come to him. Instead, he took the ewe lamb that belonged to the poor man and prepared it for the one who had come to him (2 Samuel 12:1-4, NIV).

This story enraged David because he thought the man was dead wrong—and even told Nathan the man must die for what he took from that poor man! He even went so far as to say the man in the story was without pity. Nathan looked at David and said, "You are the man!" If I could have been a fly on the wall, I'm sure I would have seen David's eyes widen and his jaw drop to the floor. God had pulled David's card and called him to the carpet for every evil thing he did to Uriah.

After Nathan spoke everything God told him to say, Nathan revealed David's punishment. God was going to bring calamity on David and take his wife and give her to one who was close to him. And that person would sleep with his wife in broad daylight, and not in secret, so all of Israel would see.

David contritely admitted his sin, and God forgave him and did not kill him. But God did not let the new baby survive. Even though David very much wanted the child to live, God kept His word on that subject. The boy died.

Lesson learned: not even a king, a president, a pope, a bishop, or a pastor is above God's law. He sees everything and does not like when anyone takes advantage of those that are weaker or under their authority. The other lesson: treat others the way you would want to be treated. No one would want to have their bed defiled by an adulterous interloper, so don't do it to someone else. God sees this and is displeased to divine vengeance.

8 NEHEMIAH, PROVOKED TO SLAPPING AND HAIR PULLING

In this next story, I don't know who to feel sorrier for: Nehemiah or the men he beat up. I'll let you decide after hearing the facts of the case. Nehemiah was part of the group of Jews who had been exiled from their homeland, the territory of Judah, due to ongoing disobedience by the Israelites towards God. Nehemiah was held captive in the fortified city of Susa and worked directly for King Artaxerxes as his esteemed cupbearer.

Word reached Nehemiah that all was not well back in Jerusalem regarding the remnant that was left. Because of the overthrow, the city of Jerusalem was left in ruins and the defensive walls were leveled, leaving the survivors vulnerable to even more looting and pillaging by opportunistic, anti-Semitic ne'er-do-wells of the surrounding regions. Since the Exodus, the Jews were under constant assault by their neighbors who resented them and their presence—and this mentality exists even today.

Nehemiah prayed out to God and asked for favor with the king. He understood he needed divine favor to even begin to do what he had in mind. When Nehemiah asked the king for permission to go back to his hometown to repair the crumbling walls, not only did he give him permission, he also gave him travel documents and a royal escort. God made Nehemiah's path straight!

But as soon as Nehemiah stepped foot into his city, the infiltrators immediately challenged his authority, as if Nehemiah was wrong for trying to rebuild the gates of his town. People who despised the Jews and had nefarious intentions for the city were challenging him. Those very people were Israel's enemies—spies and double-crossers who stood by and cheered when the Hebrews were exiled. But now they were trying to call the shots in matters that were none of their affair. Thankfully, Nehemiah was not a naïve nincompoop. He knew they were his enemy, no matter how helpful they pretended to be. He was having none of it.

People should take a study of how Nehemiah conducted himself in this dubious scenario. He was faced with all kinds of duplicitous, forked-tongue devils. We've all had this type of person of ill repute try to bamboozle us with their smiling face, but beware—they are just as the O'Jays song Back Stabbers[39] describes: smiling in Nehemiah's face but secretly trying to throw him under a speeding chariot. If you don't know how to handle these phonies, take a lesson from Nehemiah. His enemies were comparable to the wicked nanny in The Hand That Rocks the Cradle[40]; insidiously and surreptitiously trying to destroy the Jews from inside their own house.

Nehemiah stayed one step ahead of these devils by constantly telling God all his worries and fears. He let God fight his battles and maintained a laser focus on rebuilding the fallen walls. He had a limited amount of time and a whole lot of things to accomplish before having to report back to Susa. He wasn't going to waste precious seconds fooling with these sore losers. They were constantly trying to bait Nehemiah so he would let his guard down. But it didn't work. And the wall was rebuilt in only 52 days thanks to Nehemiah's discernment regarding these pack of wolves.

Nehemiah was always seeking to repent and please God so that he and his fellow Jews would be released from bondage to Persia. As governor for twelve years, Nehemiah rebuilt the crumbling walls, re-established order, and reactivated the holy days. He also relieved the Jews from many of the burdens the previous foreign governors had placed on them.

With all that Nehemiah did to fend off those scallywags, his uneducated or severely trusting brethren continually underestimated the treachery of their enemies. No sooner had Nehemiah left to return to Persia and the king, the gullible Jews let the fox in the henhouse—literally.

Tobiah the Ammonite was allowed to move into, of all places, a room in the house of God. He was the same man who taunted, baited, and antagonized the Jews during the entire rebuilding efforts. The minute Nehemiah returned from Susa, he quickly threw Tobiah and his belongings out of God's house. He could not believe his own people would do such a thing. He was trying to keep the enemy out, and they were inviting them in.

Not only that, the Jews resumed doing things God warned them not to do, such as ignoring the Sabbath by buying and selling instead of keeping it holy unto God. Nehemiah was so upset, he rebuked them and said, "Didn't your ancestors do the same things, so that our God brought all this calamity on us and on this city? Now you are stirring up more wrath against Israel by desecrating the Sabbath" (Nehemiah 13:18). Boy, Nehemiah was single-handedly trying to keep his people on the straight and narrow, but the dimwits did contrary actions that could potentially negate all his work and effort. Nehemiah was at his breaking point with these incorrigible people. I don't think he could take much more.

And he couldn't! Those unthinking imbeciles had finally diddled his last nerve when he learned the men had married foreign women—another no-no that God told them not to do. And just like Claudine[41] took that hairbrush to her teenage daughter's backside for being with child, Nehemiah snapped on his people. He beat them up one side and down the other. The scripture says, "I rebuked them and called curses down on them. I beat some of the men and pulled out their hair. I made them take an oath in God's name and said:

> *You are not to give your daughters in marriage to their sons, nor are you to take their daughters in marriage for your sons or for yourselves. Was it not because of marriages like these that Solomon king of Israel sinned? Among the many nations there was no king like him. He was loved by his*

God, and God made him king over all Israel, but even he was led into sin by foreign women. Must we hear now that you too are doing all this terrible wickedness and are being unfaithful to our God by marrying foreign women? (Nehemiah 13:25-27, NIV).

The book of Nehemiah is a great study of what one can do to overcome all the sabotage of an enemy. But it also shows how your own kin and loved ones can bring harm to you and your way of life by being silly and stupid. All the safety measures in the world don't work if you give the enemy the keys to your house. Nehemiah's brethren worked against his efforts at securing Jerusalem by continuing to allow outsiders in who had contempt in mind for the Jewish people. The very people wishing harm for the Jews were the same people they were giving refuge to and intermarrying. This defeats the purpose of having a defense system and is bad on every level.

Don't invite your enemy into your sanctuary and expect him not to kill you. Your demise will be your own fault. And Nehemiah was right to give his people a thwacking upside their heads: they were thoughtless to their own detriment.

9 YO WIDOW, IMMA LET YOU EAT, BUT FEED ME FIRST

This chapter's title may sound reminiscent of a pompous, sour-grapes rap star, however, it is actually something far more profound. This next story is an incredible example of faith, obedience, and unselfishness. It also shows how our loving God, always concerned for His people, transformed a "hanging-by-a-thread" widow's meager rations into "more than enough" in the midst of a severe famine.

To understand why Israel was suffering widespread famine and other hardships during this time, here is a quick synopsis of how things went to the left for Israel. A century prior when Solomon was king, he did some very stupid things God told him not to do. Although Solomon was wise, he let his longing loins rule him. Solomon could not get enough women to save his life, so he married pretty much every woman he laid eyes upon. He was as weak in this area as his dad David. Women were like potato chips to Solomon; he couldn't marry just one. He had to have all of them. But the Israelites were forewarned by Jehovah Yahweh not to marry foreign women—women who worshiped other gods. Because of Solomon's disobedience in this area and others, after his reign was over, the land of Israel was divided in two: the northern and southern kingdoms. The northern area was the kingdom of Israel and the southern area was the kingdom of Judah. Each region had their own independent monarch. The descendants of King David ruled the territory of Judah, and an assortment of various kings ruled the territory of Israel. And now back to our story at hand.

Elijah the prophet was sent by God to warn the king of the northern kingdom of Israel that his sins had made God mad. King Ahab and his fiendish foreign wife Jezebel wickedly attempted to outlaw the worship of the one true God by instituting mandatory, kingdom-wide Baal worship. This demonic duo continuously and flagrantly inflicted evil on the people, and at the same time conspired evil against their most vulnerable citizens. Many people went astray and lost faith in God while others lost their will to live. To get Ahab to stop his evil behavior, God withheld the rains and caused a severe drought. He instructed Elijah His prophet to proclaim to the king that not a drop of rain or dew would touch the land for the next few years. But it didn't stop foolish Ahab, and it really irked Jezebel that Elijah spoke so boldly to her husband.

After all, Jezebel was the puppet-master and driving force behind the king. God knew who and what she really was. Jezebel was from a long line of wicked Baal believers and was doing her absolute Maleficent[42] best to turn Israel away with her. She plotted and schemed worse than The Wizard of Oz's[43] Wicked Witch of the West. But Elijah obediently and bravely delivered God's prophecy as instructed. Directly afterwards, God sent Elijah into Witness Protection[44] to lay low and out of harm's way from crazy, cruel Jezebel. While at this undisclosed location near the Jordan River, ravens fed Elijah meat every morning and bread every evening. God also provided him drinking water from a nearby brook. But ultimately, the Water Runs Dry[45] from lack of rain.

God told His faithful servant Elijah, "Go to the region of Sidon" and visit a widow who would provide him with food. How wonderful of God to look out for Elijah. The only problem: God did not tell the despondent and impoverished widow any of this. She was a single mother unable to keep her and her son's head above water, much less support a stranger and unidentified traveler who just showed up out of the blue. And she was now responsible for another mouth to feed and doesn't know him from a hole in the wall.

On top of all that, as if life wasn't hard enough, she was a suicidal widow with nothing left to live for and was in the process of putting her affairs in order. She was not in the mood to play hostess with the mostest. She was literally preparing her and her son's last meal to eat, then to die. Having only enough food for one last meal, and in pitiful despair, she was going to go gently into that good night. Elijah's unannounced pop-over was the last thing she wanted or needed right now. In fact, the down-and-out bread-nabber Jean Valjean in Les Misérables[46] had more hope than this widow, and Elijah wanted to use the last of her meager ingredients to feed him first!

God was showing His grace and mercy to this widow through Elijah, which is precisely why God told him to go there. Although Elijah needed her for sustenance, she urgently needed what Elijah had even more. The widow needed her faith restored, and Elijah was faith personified. It was by God's divine mercy that softened the widow's heart to help Elijah. So Elijah assured this woman by saying, "Don't be afraid. Go home and do as you have said. But first make a small loaf of bread for me from what you have and bring it to me, and then make something for yourself and your son. For this is what the Lord, the God of Israel says: 'The jar of flour will not be used up and the jug of oil will not run dry until the day the Lord sends rain on the land'" (1 Kings 17:13-14, NIV).

This was a lot for anyone to believe at face value. She would have to trust Elijah with her very life to move forward with his demands. And that's exactly what she did. She trusted what he said. The alternative: she would have had no last measly meal and would continue on with her plans to die. Either way, she was no worse off than before. If all she had was one small loaf, there really was not any change other than Elijah would be eating it instead of her and her son. And since he was so persistent that he gets fed first, and she was too depressed to argue, why not give it to him? If nothing else, it would be a valuable lesson to Elijah if she died. Perhaps he would think twice about taking food from down-on-their-luck widows in the future.

But true to Elijah's words given to him by God Almighty, the widow's jar of flour and jug of oil did not run dry.

There was enough food for all three of them every day. What a miracle to behold. A bottomless reserve of food all because she trusted the man of God. And the widow and her son were sustained and did not die.

But out of the blue, the son fell ill and stopped breathing. The widow was anguished and asked Elijah what was the purpose for him coming there as the man of God if he was going to allow her sins to overtake her and her family. Perhaps she thought something she did caused her son to die, but that was most certainly not the case. Yet again, doubt and unbelief began to overtake her mind and heart. But as we've already witnessed, Elijah was a Man of Steel[47] in his faith and would not allow the widow to fall back into suicidal despair.

Through his faith, Elijah was able to bring her boy back to life by calling on God and laying on top of him three times. Elijah delivered a living and breathing boy back to his mother. Now she truly believed that Elijah was a man of God and the word of the Lord from his mouth was the truth. God allowed this faithless widow to come near to tragedy and suffering to redeem her from all of them. This is God's method of showing Himself as all-powerful to His people. Otherwise, when people only see bleak and hopelessness without triumph and victory, they give up. When her food did not run out and her son did not die, God proved every time He is The Great I Am. And unequivocally Superior to the Dumb and Dumber[48] pair, Jezebel and her faux god Baal—a useless piece of deadwood.

Not to be missed: both the widow and the wicked Jezebel were from Sidon, and like Jezebel, the widow likely worshiped Baal. Neither one had a relationship with nor believed in the God of Israel. That's why the widow was hopelessly willing to go gently into that good night. God used Elijah to introduce her to His abounding love and mercy. As a byproduct of his faith, he was full of God's resurrection power, which ultimately saved her son. Elijah was God's tool, sent to show the widow that the Almighty Creator of heaven and earth was alive, willing, and well able to help her in times of trouble. The lesson to remember: the sun will rise, seasons will change, and troubles will come. But God will rescue us from our difficulties. All He asks is that we graciously accept Him and His Son, so He can deliver us.

The second, almost imperceptible lesson is what God was doing to Elijah. Sending Elijah to a downhearted widow required him to walk the walk and talk the talk. The purpose: to re-energize and fortify his faith. Faith, which is trusting and relying on God, is much like a muscle. And muscles need exercise to increase their strength and endurance, especially for times when a minor trial morphs into a hardship or becomes unexpectedly protracted. In our next story, the wicked Jezebel, aka Cruella de Vil[49], becomes Elijah's trial of the century. He would need the same faith and tenacity as Rocky Balboa in all the Rocky Series[50] combined to get him through her deadly, despicable deeds. So stay tuned.

10 ELIJAH, RUNDOWN AND BURNED OUT

When we left off in our last chapter, we examined how God was taking care of two birds with one stone: showing love, mercy, and favor to The Sad Sack[51] widow while simultaneously strengthening Elijah's faith. As previously stated, faith is like a muscle and must be exercised often. When tough times Suddenly[52] come, it is vital to pull the faith parachute straightaway. Do not try to "take a go at it" yourself, or call a friend or a neighbor, unless his name is Jesus Christ, our Lord and Savior. "Faith testing" is to ingrain within you how to automatically and without hesitation trust, rely, and lean on God. Your faith is activated by simply giving the problem over to Him and maintaining your peace while He fixes it. However, this does not apply to self-inflicted repercussions due to habitual and willful disobedience. God is, or has been, trying to correct you, and now He's touching your circumstances.

In Elijah's case, he was not only obedient, he was God's soldier. Every order God gave him was performed to His exact specification. And Elijah did unbelievably brave and heroic deeds in devotion to God Almighty. After Elijah's three-year mission holed up with the hopeless widow ended, he went back to face King Ahab on a new assignment. God wanted henpecked Ahab to know that He was allowing the rain to come back (1 Kings 18:1-2). Before we go further with what happened next, let me inform you of what Ahab's bloodthirsty wife Jezebel did.

According to Obadiah, a devout believer in Jehovah Yahweh, Jezebel systematically targeted and killed God's prophets while Elijah was off the grid. Her malicious intent was to exterminate all of God's prophets to enforce Baal worship, unchallenged. Perhaps figuring if she exterminated God's representatives, it would incapacitate God. Not so fast, Beavis and Butthead[53]! This is what Almighty God had to say about her ineffectual and pernicious plans: "Do not be deceived, God is not mocked [He will not allow Himself to be ridiculed, nor treated with contempt nor allow His precepts to be scornfully set aside]; for whatever a man sows, this and this only is what he will reap" (Galatians 6:7, AMP). Now run and tell that, Jezebel.

Fresh from convalescence, Elijah's faith muscles were now the size of Popeye's[54] arms—anvils and all. He was so tanked up with faith, in one single day he diced up 450 Baal prophets after utterly embarrassing them in a "Who's god is more powerful" contest. In one day, Elijah did superhuman acts: without an army, he boldly put an end to all those phony baloney Baal prophets. Here is how it went down:

After climbing up Mt. Carmel to meet King Ahab, an intensely laborious chain of events ensued. The first was an hours-long duel of the deities. And as expected, Jehovah Yahweh remained undefeated. Brokeback[55] Baal couldn't even get the bat off his shoulders. But what would one expect from a non-god? Once and for all, Elijah proved to the flaky, fence-riding Israelites who waffled between belief in Yahweh and belief in Baal, how Baal was a dud and that God is The Great I Am.

Revealing to all of Israel that Baal worship was a bogus deception was not the end of Elijah's activities and heroism. The second thing Elijah did was more exhausting than John Wick's[56] fight scenes. To ensure the matter of Baal was kaput, Elijah seized the Baal hooligans, transported them to the nearby Kishon brook, then lacerated them to death. Elijah took no prisoners in this all-day Battle Royale[57]. Afterwards, without so much as a 20-minute power nap or a Gatorade, Elijah ran 17 miles to the town of Jezreel. He ran so fast he outran the imminent precipitation, as well as Ahab's chariot despite its head start.

When gutless Ahab finally reached Jezreel, like a servile Stepford Wife, he reported to Jezebel what Elijah had done to her prophets. Enraged, she sent word to Elijah stating, "May the gods strike me dead if by this time tomorrow I don't take your life the way you took the lives of Baal's prophets" (1 Kings 19:2, GW). So much for Elijah taking a relaxing hot liniment bath after this grueling day. There would be no rest for this extremely weary prophet as long as Jezebel was on the hunt.

Fearing for his life, Elijah tucked in his tunic and ran like Forrest Gump[58] all the way to Beersheba in the southern territory of Judah. It was over 260 miles, and Elijah was already depleted from fighting Baal. And now he's cross-country running all over God's creation. The Bible makes no mention of him eating on his long-haul run, so without a doubt he's heading for a severe system crash. The only thing that saved Elijah was God's messengers who provided him with bread and water. Along with some restorative sleep, this food refueled him enough to continue travel all the way to Mount Sinai—another 200 miles south.

Elijah ran all this way in fear, and now he was begging God to allow him to die. Jezebel's relentless threats, coupled with her compulsive desire to murder, had sent him into a state of deep depression. His mind became overtaken by the same affliction of dread and futility— much like the unfortunate widow he brought back from the doorstep of death. Although Elijah reinforced his faith during his visit with the widow, he also succumbed to the oppression he felt from Jezebel's unyielding evil. Compounded by not eating, not drinking water, and not getting adequate sleep, it's no surprise his mind and body could not defend itself against the hostile takeover of the discouraging and thriving evils all around him. That's exactly why God's word says, "a person cannot live on bread alone, but on every word that the LORD speaks" (Deut 8:3, GW).

The lessons learned here should be obvious but are very often taken for granted by the average, complacent young person. First and foremost, we are human beings, not machines. As homo sapiens, which is Latin for "wise man," we must eat enough food for our bodies to work properly. That means drink enough water to stay hydrated and get adequate rest to renew our minds. A body that is deprived, depleted, or overworked is no good for anything or to anyone. A tired and weary mind is easy prey for psychosis. An invigorated mind and body can withstand even extreme conditions when it is continuously affixed to God's word.

Secondly, all the faith strengthening in the world won't help when your mind is "LO CELL"—depleted, running on fumes, drained. As soon as Elijah heard the vicious report from Jezebel, his mind failed to recall how to give his worries over to God. Again, this was a direct result of his lack of mental cognition from overexertion. The mind and body must be recharged. John 14:26, AMPC tells us:

> The Holy Spirit, Whom the Father will send in My name [in My place, to represent Me and act on My behalf], He will teach you all things. And He will cause you to recall (will remind you of, bring to your remembrance) everything I have told you.

But if the mind and body are frayed and broken down, how can God bring anything to your remembrance? Take care of your mind and body like the precious gifts they are. Because once they're gone, they're gone for good.

Lastly, no matter how full of energy, zest, and resurrection faith you possess, at the first inkling of anxiety—and at all other times—give all your worries and cares to God. Don't try to handle the little things and give the really big things to God. This method of "doing God" can backfire as one starts to become overly reliant on their own talents, skills, and abilities. Victory over life's struggles, difficulties, and pitfalls is directly related to dependence on God and not yourself.

Map 5. Elijah's Overtaxing Trip

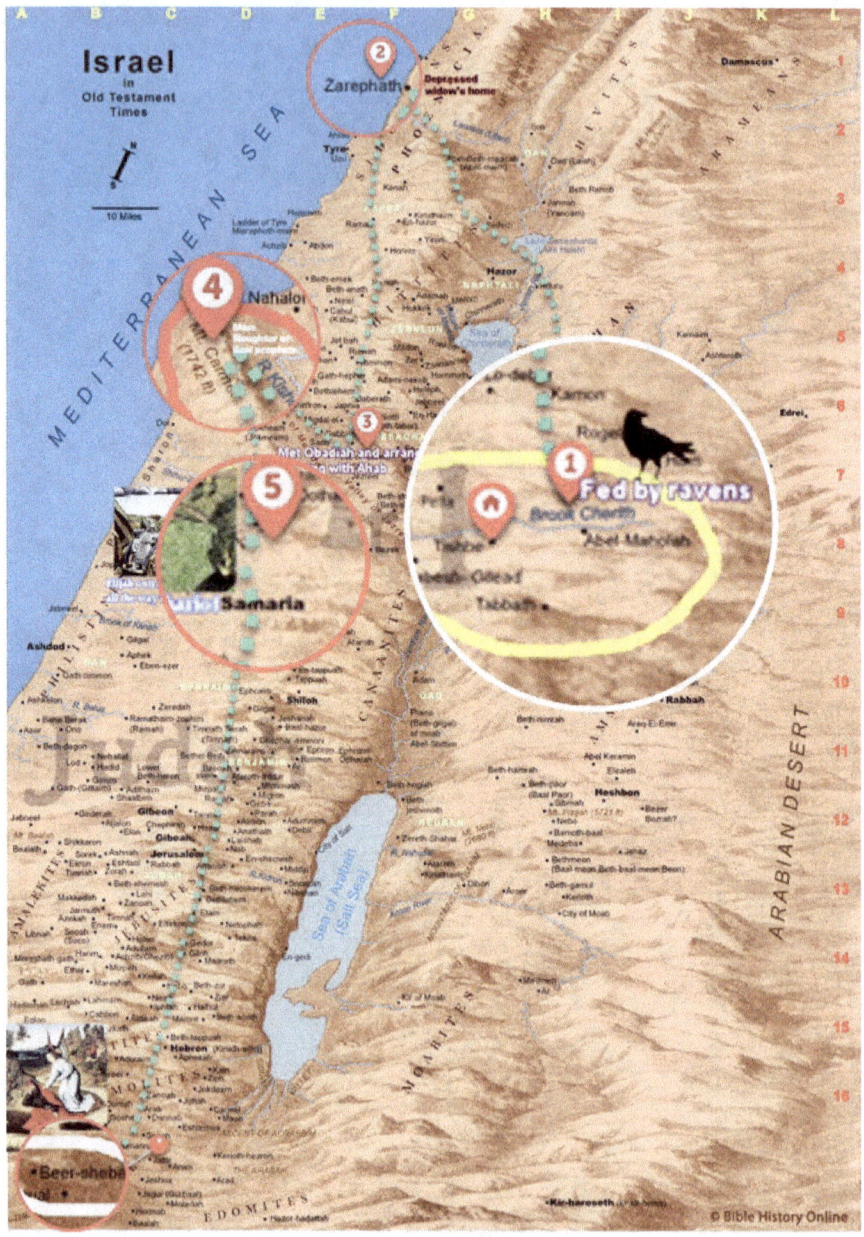

Map 1. *Source* http://www.bible-history.com/geography/ancient-israel-old-testament.html *Accessed: 11/28/2017*

11 SAMSON: PILLOW TALK WITH TWO-FACED FEMALES WILL BE YOUR RUIN

The book of Judges recounts the condition of the Hebrews after they eventually made it to the promised land of Canaan. Moses was already resting in paradise and Joshua, his successor, very recently went the way of his forefathers too. It is important to understand just how blessed the Hebrews were when Moses and Joshua led them. The people prospered because their leaders feared and reverently obeyed God. God's anointing was so strongly upon them, they conquered all the nations around them with supernatural ease.

But once Joshua died, his leadership that commanded them to choose a path was gone too. Joshua's "no nonsense, say it to your face" style of leadership helped keep the hardheaded heathens in check. Moses was often exasperated to exhaustion by them. But Joshua didn't play those games. He told those flip-flopping backsliders, "...But if serving the Lord seems undesirable to you, then choose for yourselves this day whom you will serve, whether the gods your ancestors served beyond the Euphrates, or the gods of the Amorites in whose land you are living. But as for me and my household, we will serve the Lord" (Joshua 24:15, NIV). Joshua was letting them know he was not like Moses and would not tolerate any wavering from them. He was so resolute in his love and obedience to God, he was ready, willing, and prepared to cut ties with them over any foolishness, especially disobedience against God Almighty. And while he was alive, they did not forsake their God.

But sadly, because many of the elders had not taught their children to fear God and walk in His ways, within a short time of Joshua's death, the younger Israelites began worshipping other gods and doing evil in the eyes of the Lord. Much like their stiff-necked ancestors, the favor, blessings, and prosperity from God was flippantly and thoughtlessly rejected. They instead chose the ephemeral support of the very nations who ultimately enslaved them. And as a learning lesson, God allowed this to happen to them Time After Time[59]. Otherwise, how else would they learn?

There were twelve judges during this roughly 400-year span who were common, ordinary people full of flaws who took a leadership stance against oppression inflicted by the surrounding nations. Whenever the Israelites would fall away from God and unfaithfully follow after other nations, God's word inevitably came to pass. Those nations would soon oppress the Israelites and bring them into vassal or servitude subjugation. Once the recalcitrant Hebrews figured out they caused all this trouble for themselves, they would repent and cry out to God. God would lift up and anoint a judge who would deliver a staggering blow against whatever oppressor happened to be tormenting them at the time, delivering the forgetful Hebrews and finally bringing about a long or short period of peace. Lather, rinse, and repeat.

And Samson, The Incredible Hulk[60] Nazarite, was the last of the judges. The other judges in order were Othniel, Ehud, Shamgar, Deborah, Gideon, Tola, Jair, Jephthah, Ibzan, Elon, and Abdon. Samson had incredible strength as a result of A) God's anointing and B) his hair. A Nazarite is dedicated to God from the womb. While Samson's mom was pregnant, she was not allowed to drink wine or other fermented drink or eat anything unclean. Samson had all the same restrictions and also one more: he must never ever cut his hair. As a matter of fact, the Bible describes his hair as seven braids.

Samson knew the source of his strength was his hair. Unfortunately, he failed to recognize the source of his weakness: his loose lips.

Samson was a young "know it all." And when he became of age, he wanted things without any delays. His parents tried to make helpful suggestions that would be wiser for him, like finding a woman among his own people instead of a Philistine woman who did not know or love God. But Samson was hardheaded and demanded exactly what he wanted. With his He-Man[61] strength, I doubt his elderly parents wanted to deal with his overgrown Bamm-Bamm Rubble from the Flintstones[62] temper tantrums.

Like good overprotective parents, they chaperoned their son to Timnah, where his must-have bride lived. At some point on the way, Samson was almost the prey of a roaring lion who happened to be roaming near the vineyards of Timnah. Judges 14:6 says, "The Spirit of the Lord came powerfully upon him so that he tore the lion apart with his bare hands as he might have torn a young goat." Not missing a beat or telling his parents, he went to the woman and decided he indeed liked her, and she would be his wife.

On his way back to Timnah to claim his bride, Samson came upon the carcass of the lion he had slaughtered. He saw that honeybees had placed their honey in this most unusual host. Compelled by stark stupidity, Samson scooped out some honey for himself, then shared it with his parents. He never told his parents that they had eaten honey from this most unclean thing. Samson had violated the conditions of being a Nazarite given by God. But this would not be his only stupid mistake that would bring him closer and closer to his ultimate ruin.

At his seven-day wedding feast attended by the male relatives of his betrothed, Samson the simpleton told a riddle. Perhaps he wanted to sound smart or look intelligent, so he even added an incentive wager. If they guessed the correct answer, he would give them 30 linen garments and 30 sets of clothes. If they could not, they would have to give those things to him. The men became frustrated when they could not figure out Samson's riddle, so they threatened his fiancée and told her they would burn her and her father's household to death if she did not explain the riddle. Feeling the pressure, she began to conspire against Samson to save her own hide.

She sobbed and told Samson that he must not really love her because he had not told her the answer. He told her, I haven't told anyone the answer, not even my parents. She continued crying and finally wore him out, and he told her. As expected, she betrayed him tout suite and told those that had threatened her. I don't know why he was surprised, if at all. But he was certainly fuming when they told him the answer. He barked, "If you had not plowed with my heifer, you would not have solved my riddle" (Judges 14:18). He should have been mad at himself. He was the idiot who had to have the foreign wife he knew absolutely nothing about. And he was the one that offered up that stupid wager he couldn't afford to lose because he didn't have the money in the first place.

His stupid bet went Sideways[63] in so many ways. Not only did he lose the bet, his wife was given to another man after Samson left to go get the loot he owed. However, God did allow Samson to strike down 30 Philistine men from Ashkelon. How else would Samson get those clothes he never had? This mass killing and Samson's later revenge, which will be discussed in the next chapter, were all divinely orchestrated by God. When Samson initially told his parents he wanted a

Philistine woman, the scripture placed in parentheses this statement: "His parents did not know that this was from the Lord, who was seeking an occasion to confront the Philistines; for at that time they were ruling over Israel" (Judges 14:4).

Remember "Judgy Judah"? Well, Samson was also a man with flaws, just as all of us have. The flaws that tripped up Samson were: he talked way too much and divulged secrets to a woman who was clearly not trustworthy. He also made wagers he could not afford. Lastly and most importantly, he took for granted the wonderful and good gift that God had given him since birth. By eating the honey from an unclean dead carcass, he was violating the covenant between himself and God. But rest assured, God can use our mistakes for His good purposes. Thankfully, God is very slow to anger, because Samson was obtuse and liked to push the envelope. In the next chapter, see how he spills the beans and sabotages himself once again.

Darnnell Reese

12 WILDFIRES, A JAWBONE AND PILLARS: WEAPONS OF MASS DESTRUCTION

In our last story, we left off with Samson losing a wager after his soon-to-be wife sold him out to her people. And to pony up, he went to a town of Philistines and killed 30 men and took their garments. If nothing else, Samson paid his debts. He was an honorable cold-blooded murderer, but he did not welch on a bet. With his newly acquired threads, he headed back to collect his wife. After all, it wasn't her fault those brutish Philistine men threatened to kill her and her father's household if she didn't divulge the answer to Samson's riddle. Again, oversharing was Samson's weakness, not hers. Unfortunately, when Samson arrived, his father-in-law would not even open the door. He had the nerve to give his wife to another man. After all the stuff he had to deal with, murdering innocent men to pay his debt, now he doesn't even have a wife. Unapologetically, his father-in-law did offer his younger daughter to Samson as a consolation prize. Feeling quite Deceived[64], this was the straw that broke the camel's back.

108

Samson decided he would exact revenge on these damned dirty Philistines. Thinking like a true Psycho[65], Samson tied up 300 foxes by the tails in pairs. He fastened torches to each pair, then lit the torches. Ablaze and scorching, the frantic and flaming foxes ran through the Philistines' crops, vineyards, and groves, burning down everything (See Judges 15:1-5). Only the mind of a twisted madman would think of something that Savage[66], no matter how effective it was. But Samson was known to eat from the guts of rotting roadkill, so what else should we have expected from him? He hasn't been working with a full deck from Day One[67].

Going tit for tat, the Philistines decided to do to Samson's ex what they had threatened to do in the first place. They burned her and her father to death. This was retribution for the Firefox[68] prank started by Samson. I'm starting to realize why Samson had to go so hard on these foolish Philistines. Samson had to behave and think just as revoltingly and unreasonably as they did. They were not civilized in the slightest. Therefore, God wanted to eradicate them. Remember, this was God's plan in the first place. God wanted a reason to confront these Beastly[69] tormenters because they were oppressing His people. But they met their match with Samson. They got the right one, baby.

Not backing down after they incinerated his ex and her dad, Samson retaliated with a vicious takedown, killing even more of them. With the exchanges between Samson and the Philistines now at its boiling point, Samson decided to lay low in a cave in Etam, in the territory of Judah, until tensions cooled. But the riled rulers would not relent. Hot on Samson's trail, they camped out near him in Lehi, frightening the poor Israelites who lived there. But the Philistines were only there to get Samson. That was all they wanted. Relieved, the fearful and dispirited Israelites swiftly went to Samson, tied him up, and carried him off to his awaiting pursuers. They had no misgivings about handing over a flamboyant macho-man with a penchant for foreign women. But don't forget who and what Samson was. He was Israel's judge with the Spirit of God in him. And this was God's doing. When God is running the show, you never know just how events will unfold. However, one thing's for certain: there would be shock and awe.

Without warning, "the Spirit of the Lord came powerfully upon him" (Judges 15:14). As if they were dried-out rubber bands, Samson effortlessly snapped the ropes on his arms. And like a real O.G., No Holds Barred[70], Old School[71] fighter, Samson grabbed the jawbone of a donkey carcass lying on the ground and skillfully wielded it as a weapon of mass destruction. Bludgeoning and beating to death a thousand of those persistent oppressive oppressors. What an awesome display of Uncommon Valor[72]! The Spirit of Almighty God was unleashed on those terrible tyrants in the same manner as a nuclear explosion. Samson's Fist of Fury[73] thrashing of Israel's enemy was a pivotal event. It ended the tyranny of the Philistines and brought with it sustained peace to the Hebrews for the next 20 years. Nothing could bring strongman Samson down.

Well, let's not overlook Samson's more dubious traits. He may have been Israel's judge, but that doesn't make him a saint in the least. He was a known oversharer with a taste for foreign females, spiteful and vengeful. True, but how could those minor faults cause any harm? I'm glad you asked. For anyone naïve enough to discount the amount of damage a loose-lip, pleasure-seeking, reckless, hotheaded, vindictive person can cause, please pay careful attention. Soon enough, his questionable personality traits amounted to the costliest liability thus far, for himself and possibly for the future stability of Israel as well.

During a trip to Gaza, in Philistine territory, Samson observed a prostitute among the town's people and spent the evening with her. Here Samson was, boldly fornicating with and among the very people he deposed, without a concern in the world. This was not a healthy place for him to be. But his nature trumped his judgment at that moment. And while he was preoccupied with fleshly fulfillment, the men of the town lay in wait for him overnight at the city gate. Presuming Samson would either gullibly or obliviously walk back through the gates, they set out to ambush him. But the foolish Philistines failed to factor in how devious Samson was. Samson's mind was much like theirs. He could match treachery with them all day long. And somehow, some way, Samson discerned an ambush was plotted against him and nimbly left the brothel in the middle of the night. When he got to the city gates, he ripped the gates off its foundation and carried the entire structure to the top of a hill. Another antagonizing blow to the Philistines, right in their own town. That'll teach them not to plot against Samson.

But just as vengeful as Samson was, so too were these fat-headed Philistines. They were now burning with rage and fueled by visions of a big Payback[74][75] and could not let their vendettas go.

Why, oh Why Do Fools Fall in Love[76]? As fate or folly would have it, Samson's nature led him to the arms of yet another Philistine woman by the name of Delilah. At this juncture, I must disabuse you of any false notions that Samson and Delilah[77] is or was the greatest love story ever told, if that is in fact what you believed. It is far from a tale of innocence and burgeoning young love. It's more of the same old Samson: a lustful man with a partiality for Poison Ivy's[78] and prostitutes who are quick to sell his bean-spilling buttocks to the highest bidder. And true to his nature, he stuck to his nonsensical thought process that permitted him to foolishly divulge the secrets of his God-given anointing.

Ever deceitful, Delilah from the Sorek Valley nagged Samson nonstop to tell her the source of his strength. Any person with eyeballs would know she was tricking him and didn't care for him in the least. Except for simple Samson, that is. But to Samson's credit, he tried to dodge Delilah by feeding her a string of tall tales and

Bedtime Stories[79] regarding his strength. Without fail, after every one of Samson's false confessions, dastardly Delilah forwarded the fake news to the Philistines like a whistleblower on WikiLeaks. And within hours, an ambush party would appear "by chance" and attempt to restrain him using the bogus takedown tactic he had fallaciously fed to his sneaky seductress. Women were truly his weakness, which is why he ultimately and unwisely told her the real truth behind his strength.

Unbelievable! The loose-lipped lion killer strikes again and blabbed everything to Delilah: "Because I am a Nazarite, no one has ever cut the hair on my head. I was dedicated to God before I was born. If my hair is ever shaved off, my strength will leave me. Then I'll be like any other man" (Judges 16:17). Is Samson a simpleton, or is he just plain stupid? Within a New York Minute[80], deceptive Delilah put the quixotic Samson to sleep then had her goons shave his head. While he was utterly defenseless, she duplicitously divulged Samson's secrets to his arch enemies. Betraying her gullible boyfriend netted this She-Devil[81] 5,500 pieces of silver. But it's not like Samson didn't have a plethora of warnings and opportunities to flee this fake friendship, but no. He chose to ignore the blaring alarm bells of Delilah's Sinister[82] ways.

Either way, Samson played himself. And now those sore losers pounced on his lack of judgment and swiftly began to avenge all of Samson's previous deeds when he made a mockery of them. The first thing they did was gouge out his eyes. (What is up with these people? They love to gouge out eyeballs. Remember how they threatened to gouge out only the right eyes of the Israelites in chapter 5, and the people cried out to King Saul? But I digress; now back to Samson.) Then they dragged him back to Gaza and imprisoned him. Yes, the same Gaza he cavorted with the prostitute and dragged their city gates up a high hill like he was in The World's Strongest Man contest. Sad and sightless, Samson was placed into forced labor and tied down with two sets of chains. They were taking no chances with this anointed man of God.

Prematurely sacrificing to their faux god Dagon, these dopey Philistines started dancing and prancing at the defeat and capture of Samson. All the Philistine rulers attended this spectacle, along with over three thousand men and women who also watched from the roof of the building. They sang:

> *"Our god gave our enemy, destroyer of our land and killer of so many, into our very hand!"*

Unfortunately, they celebrated a little too soon. The dumb Philistines failed to look five seconds into the future and postulate on Samson's hair growing back. Duh! What ignoramus doesn't know hair grows back?! And Samson's hair started growing back as soon as it was shaved off. Proof that you can't keep a good man down.

Trying to further embarrass Samson, they brought him out to be the blind and bound buffoon at this unholy celebration. But stubborn Samson, God's anointed lion slayer, would give them a show to die for—literally. Samson's obsessive resolution for retribution was on full tilt. He asked God to allow him to pay them back for at least one of his eyes. This was how Samson rolled, all day every day. He was not going to let their violent eye enucleation go without Bringing Down the House[83]. He prayed out to God for the last ounce of strength needed to kill all those doomed and detestable Philistines. While praying and pushing with all his might against their support pillars, he asked God to let him die with them. Samson triumphantly collapsed the entire building down on the heads of the Philistines, killing the rulers and all the goggling gawkers too. And yes, Samson also went down in a Blaze of Glory[84] [85].

The awesome lesson learned here was of Samson's courageous character. He should not be censoriously judged; rather, he should be celebrated. He was as right as rain in God's eyes. His tenacious nature was constant, and probably very refreshing to God. Fickle fence riders are useless and repulsive to God. Revelation 3:16 tells us to either be cold or hot, but not lukewarm or God will spew you out of His mouth. Samson did and behaved exactly how God called him to be: a thorn in the Philistines' side; salt in their open wounds; vinegar in their eyes. God was seeking an occasion to do something against the Philistines, and in this situation, he was The Best Man[86] for the job.

Sure, Samson was immature and reckless, but the bottom line was that Samson was an authentic, unapologetic, strong-willed leader who avidly defended himself and his people from those who dared to oppress them. Moreover, he was God's anointed because he was unafraid of man or beast. God can work with this type of person because of their courageous heart. Scared, timid, or overthinking people will sometimes hesitate when God needs them to act. Samson moved and acted without hesitation or fear. We all should ask God for this type of courage in similar situations. It is a welcomed attribute in the body of Christ.

Map 6. Samson's Violent Vocations

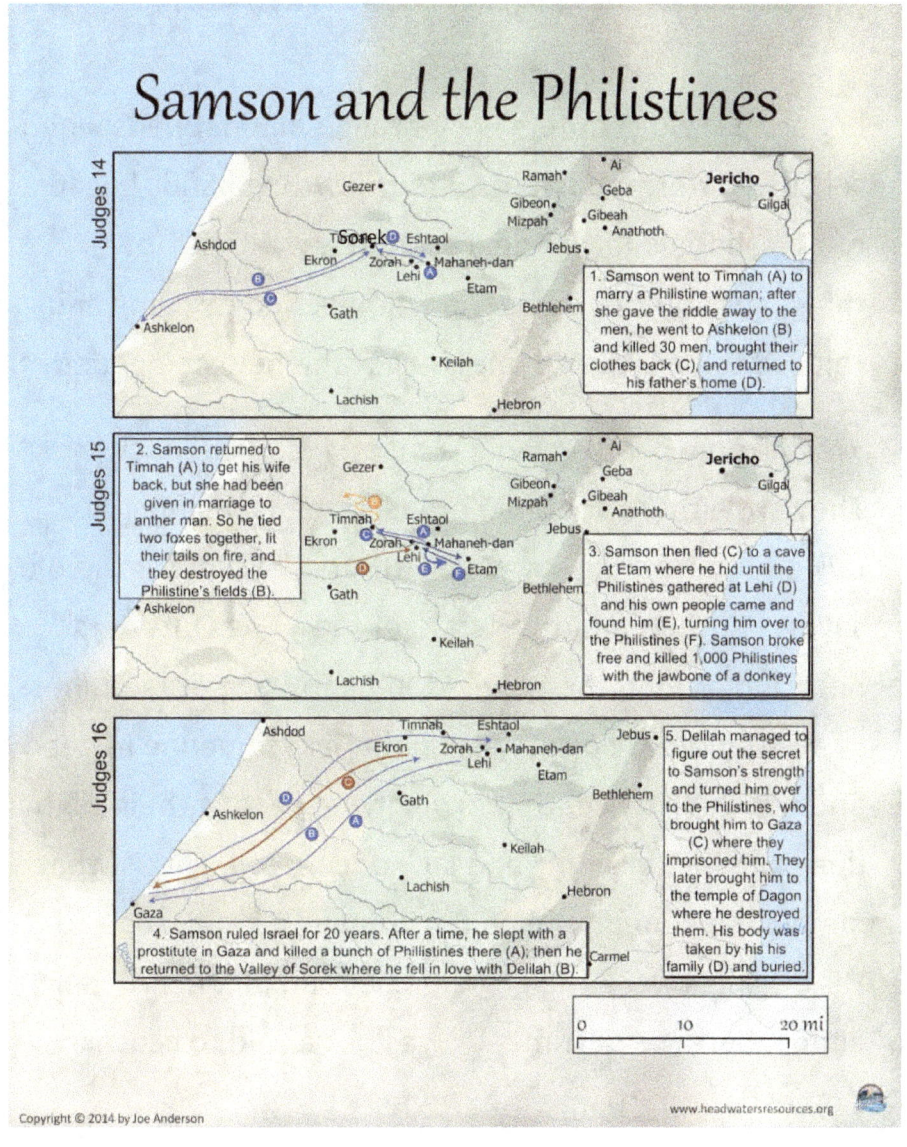

Source: http://www.headwaterresources.org Accessed 4/9/2018

13 PEOPLE HATE WHEN YOU MAKE A SCENE FOR JESUS, BUT HE LOVES IT

In our last two chapters we learned what happens when sensitive information gets into the wrong hands because of oversharing. In this next scenario, we'll see how things turn out for someone who needed rescuing and refused to be silenced until he got the help he needed.

We all know people who are quiet, reserved, or shy. They are either very timid or just don't have much to talk about. Nothing's wrong with that, except for the old saying: "Closed mouths don't get fed." The Outsiders[87] near and around them who don't know the dreadfulness of a situation will often walk right past someone in need and not think twice. Unknowingly neglecting their plight due to their Oblivion[88] and lack of concern. This is what almost happened to Blind Bartimaeus when Jesus and His disciples were walking along a road in Jericho. I said almost because Bartimaeus was not afraid to cause a Domestic Disturbance[89].

Bartimaeus was like most Tramps[90] or panhandlers loitering in busy bazaars or areas where they might meet a kind and generous person. These people are not hurting anyone just because they shake their money cups or wave those handwritten cardboard signs. They need money and are making sure you see them. This is what they do to survive, and I say more power to them. God bless them because they are trying. Unfortunately, after a while, people tend to ignore them and become desensitized to their poverty. Probably thinking they are hustlers who are just trying to get over—not willing to work and taking the easy way out. But that is not the case in this situation.

For example, Bartimaeus lived in a time without reasonable accommodations for individuals with physical disabilities such as blindness. Anyone who had a physical disability most likely was rendered useless or possibly not regarded whatsoever. And in all likelihood, Bartimaeus was overlooked because he was a regular fixture sitting on the side of the road begging. People saw him yet didn't see him all at the same time. However, this particular day would be the day Bartimaeus, like Glenn Close in Fatal Attraction[91], would violently declare, "I'm Not Going to be IGNORED, Dan!"

The reason Bartimaeus became so amplified is easy to understand. He was sick and tired of being cast aside and ignored because people only saw him as a blind and broke beggar. And everyone around him was yammering on and on about the man of God walking all over Israel healing people just like him. This was too good to be true, but Bartimaeus was determined that if he ever got the chance to meet Jesus, come Hell or High Water[92], he was going to get Jesus to give him his sight.

Thankfully, Bartimaeus was blind and not deaf. When his once-in-a-lifetime moment happened and he heard the voices of Jesus and His disciples nearby, he began to shout at the top of his lungs, "JESUS, SON OF DAVID, HAVE MERCY ON ME!" (Mark 10:46, NIV). The gift of sight is worth fighting for. And now Bartimaeus is within a stone's throw away from his gift. Not only was Bartimaeus shouting for Jesus, he was shouting from pure panic. This was all he ever wanted, and he was not going to let it go without a fight. Anyone else would have done the exact same thing. So when the people tried to shush Bartimaeus, he would not comply. In fact, he defiantly shouted even louder: "SON OF DAVID, HAVE MERCY ON ME!"

Bartimaeus's bellowing certainly got Jesus's attention and compelled Him to stop and call him over to Him.

This was Bartimaeus's "come to Jesus moment," and he was determined to be heard. Jesus's million-dollar question to Bartimaeus was, "What do you want me to do for you?" Bartimaeus could have flubbed under the pressure, stuttered or stammered miserably, but it would not have mattered to Jesus. Jesus loves people and desires to help all who ask. Similar to a Madea[93] reprimand, Bartimaeus clearly pronounced every syllable when he articulated, "Rabbi, I-want-to-see." You can't get any clearer than that. Bartimaeus wanted his basic ability to see. And because he boldly asked for what he desired on the strength of what he had been told about Jesus, he was healed in that very instant when Jesus said, "Go, your faith has healed you."

The amazing and beautiful lesson from Blind Bartimaeus is to never ever let anyone shush or silence you when you need help. These people can't possibly know what you need or don't need, so who are they to tell you to be quiet and not speak up? They are unaware adversaries at best, or undermining conspirators at worst, and you are not bound to listen to them for any reason. You are a child of The Most High God, and He has redeemed you for Himself. So boldly come forward, Raise Your Voice[94], and tell God what you want, what you need, and how you feel. He cares, and He will listen and make a change in your situation if that's what you're asking for. Just like He did for the woman who was bleeding, the Centurion's sick servant, the royal official's son, Jairus's daughter, and so many others who boldly came to Him for healing. Jesus did it for them, and He will do it for you.

14 JESUS SHARPSHOOTER OF THE TRUTH

Although Jesus was without sin, this by no means suggests he was indulgent or appeasing. Hebrews 4:12-13 correctly and descriptively states:

> *"His powerful Word is sharper than any two-edged sword and cuts as deep as the place where soul and spirit meet, the place where joints and marrow meet."*

His truth does indeed sting, but just as important, it is darn funny. His words are so painful, shocking, zapping, and exposing, gobsmacked is the best word to describe your condition after a Jesus zinger.

Let's begin with Jesus's blunt interactions with those he loved: his disciples, his family, and those who sought his healing. Then we will further amuse ourselves with his more vicious, but always truthful, castigations he spoke against the phony baloney religious hypocrisy. Keep in mind that Jesus had a lot of things to do in a short amount of time. On top of that, he was dealing with his own approaching death. He was under a tremendous amount of stress and had no time for explaining basic principles to the disciples over and over. This is why He was embarrassingly truthful with them.

In Mark 8:11, Jesus warns them about the yeast of the Pharisees. This is a perfect example of how Jesus is driven to vexation because of the inane discussions of His beloved disciples. Earlier, Jesus had performed two miraculous feedings of the people, back to back. With very little bread and only a few fish, Jesus multiplied food that would barely feed a family of three and fed over 5,000 and 4,000 men respectively. Witnessing such an event is unforgettable to say the least. So why was it that when Jesus warned His disciples to be on their guard against the yeast of the Pharisees and the Herodians, did they presume Jesus was questioning them about forgetting to take bread?

> *They had been discussing with one another that they didn't have any bread.*

> *Jesus knew what they were saying and asked them, "Why are you discussing the fact that you don't have any bread? Don't you understand yet? Don't you catch on? Are your minds closed? Are you blind and deaf? Don't you remember? When I*

broke the five loaves for the five thousand, how many baskets did you fill with leftover pieces?"

They told him, "Twelve."

"When I broke the seven loaves for the four thousand, how many large baskets did you fill with leftover pieces?"

They answered him, "Seven."

He asked them, "Don't you catch on yet?" (Mark 8:16-21, GW)

An innocent blunder by the disciples, right? However, sometimes Jesus was too allegorical for almost anyone to follow. In John 11, when Lazarus died, Jesus informed them, "Our friend Lazarus is sleeping, and I'm going to Bethany to wake him." I don't know about you, but I would not have thought any differently than they did. He talked in riddles and parables, so you never knew when He was speaking enigmatically or straightforwardly. That's why the disciples said this in John 11:12-15:

"Lord, if he's sleeping, he'll get well."

Jesus meant that Lazarus was dead, but the disciples thought Jesus meant that Lazarus was only sleeping. Then Jesus told them plainly, "Lazarus has died, but I'm glad that I wasn't there so that you can grow in faith. Let's go to Lazarus."

Yet another time when His disciples were slow to understand, Jesus had to launch his zinger slingshot once again. Jesus educated the disciples and the people truthfully of what makes a person defiled. Jesus explained this because of the hypocrisy of the Pharisees and teachers of the law. They called His disciples unclean because they had not ceremonially washed their hands before eating. With typical obtuse fashion, the disciples missed the mark on what Jesus meant. And in Mark 7:18-23 NIV, He gave it to them good:

"Are you so dull?" he asked. "Don't you see that nothing that enters a person from the outside can defile them? For it doesn't go into their heart but into their stomach, and then out of the body." (In saying this, Jesus declared all foods clean.)

He went on: "What comes out of a person is what defiles them. For it is from within, out of a person's heart, that evil thoughts come—sexual immorality, theft, murder, adultery, greed, malice, deceit, lewdness, envy, slander, arrogance and folly. All these evils come from inside and defile a person."

As you can see, Jesus is a straight shooter. He expressed what needed to be said straight up, no chaser. In this next example, you'll see how He handled people who came out to hear Him teach. Sometimes these people were not really concerned with His message but only wanted His miracles. In John 6, the account of Jesus feeding the 5,000 men with only a few loaves of bread and two fish is retold from John's point of view. The difference in John's version was the additional details of how the people were looking for Jesus on the other side of the lake. They had not seen Jesus leave with the disciples the evening before. When they all went to the other side and saw Jesus, they approached Him with an insincere and flowery, "Rabbi, when did you get here?" To which Jesus unapologetically chops them down at the shins when He said:

"You've come looking for me not because you saw God in my actions but because I fed you, filled your stomachs—and for free.

"Don't waste your energy striving for perishable food like that. Work for the food that sticks with you, food that nourishes your lasting life, food the Son of Man provides. He and what he does are guaranteed by God the Father to last."

These comical scenarios clearly demonstrate that Jesus is the Truth[95]. He may be gentle as a lamb and His yoke is light, but please don't mistake his benevolence to be synonymous with a coddling people pleaser. Case in point: when Jesus used his mouth as a double-edged sword of truth, the liars and authoritarians who were deliberate partakers reviled Him. Especially the Pharisees and Sadducees: the high-ranking members of Jewish society and teachers of the law.

These elitist autocrats hated Jesus because He was upsetting the applecart. They were influential members of Jewish society and had superior positions in the church. So when Jesus arrived on the scene and started figuratively and literally opening blind eyes and calling out their hidden and blatant hypocrisy, He became their Enemy of the State[96]. They knew it would be a matter of time before what He taught caught fire and caused an uprising. They were fearful their hold and oppression on the people would inevitably be broken. But Jesus was not inexperienced to their baits and tricks. He skillfully and boldly called them out on all their treachery. In Matthew 22:15-22 (MSG), they futilely tried to trap Jesus again. But His lexical truth laser burned white hot through these forked-tongue devils yet again:

> That's when the Pharisees plotted a way to trap him into saying something damaging. They sent their disciples, with a few of Herod's followers mixed in, to ask, "Teacher, we know you have integrity, teach the way of God accurately, are indifferent to popular opinion, and don't pander to your students. So tell us honestly: Is it right to pay taxes to Caesar or not?"

> Jesus knew they were up to no good. He said, "Why are you playing these games with me? Why are you trying to trap me? Do you have a coin? Let me see it." They handed him a silver piece. "This engraving—who does it look like? And whose name is on it?"

> They said, "Caesar."

"Then give Caesar what is his, and give God what is his."

The Pharisees were speechless. They went off shaking their heads.

This scathing lashing was only the tip of the iceberg. Throughout the entire chapter of Matthew 23, Jesus unloads with both barrels on those wicked hypocrites. He went in on them without apology regarding their pillaging of widows, their holier-than-thou attitudes, their lengthy platitudinous prayers, their endless flaunting and attention-seeking ways, and how they load everyone else with rules and regulations that they themselves don't follow.

I'm quite certain Jesus calculated the cost and knew He had nothing to lose by telling the truth to these unholy blasphemers. His purpose for being in the world was to bring salvation. And His mission didn't require Him to make friends with these evil and perverse pretenders. What He was skillfully doing was giving them a reason to put a target on His back. It was all a part of God's masterful plan to bring salvation to the world, once and for all, through the absolute sacrifice of His sinless son. Beautifully, Jesus[97] blasted these puffed-up Pharisees and Sadducees with full awareness they would be gunning for him, conspiring against Him, and would hand Him over to be killed. Undaunted, Jesus would continue His livid lecture and sink them like the Titanic[98] with His truth bombs. The following excerpts from the Gospels of Luke 20:46-47 (GW) and Matthew 23:2-7 (GW) offer only a thimbleful of the cutting reproach Jesus discharged on those flimflam artists:

> *Beware of the experts in Moses' Teachings! They like to walk around in long robes and love to be greeted in the marketplaces, to have the front seats in the synagogues and the places of honor at dinners. They rob widows by taking their houses and then say long prayers to make themselves look good. The experts in Moses' Teachings will receive the most severe punishment.*

And in Matthew:

> *The experts in Moses' Teachings and the Pharisees teach with Moses' authority. So be careful to do everything they tell you. But don't follow their example, because they don't practice what they preach. They make loads that are hard to carry and lay them on the shoulders of the people.*

However, they are not willing to lift a finger to move them. They do everything to attract people's attention. They make their headbands large and the tassels on their shawls long. They love the place of honor at dinners and the front seats in synagogues. They love to be greeted in the marketplaces and to have people call them Rabbi.

To fully appreciate Jesus's stinging rebuke, read Matthew 23. It contains the entire juicy, jaw-dropping diatribe. And Jesus breaks it down so it can forever and consistently be broke—putting those posers in their rightful place. Matthew 23 is the perfect starting point that illustrates Jesus's total lack of pretense when it comes to His Father's business.

The surpassing lesson gleaned here for all of us is: when striving to be Christ-like and doing God's work to advance His Kingdom, you must be truthful, and sometimes the truth hurts. But only for a little while. Equivocating or coddling to delicate people, the masses, the elite, the powerful, or influential will alienate you from right standing with God. Mealy-mouthed people don't represent the truth of God and are a hindrance to His Kingdom. If our Lord and Savior offended people when He spoke the truth, shouldn't we also expect to offend as well when we speak His truth? Jesus acutely warned His flock that only A Few Good Men[99] could handle the truth, but many more would fall away:

> *And then shall many be offended and shall betray one another and shall hate one another (Matthew 24:10, Jubilee).*

> *And Blessed is he who is not offended in me (Matthew 11:6, Jubilee).*

And lastly, when faced with accusers on all sides like Jesus did, pray often for His strength and courage to do all that Christ asks of us. You will surely need it in this world.

THE END

Map 7. Locations Where Jesus Walked, Healed and Preached

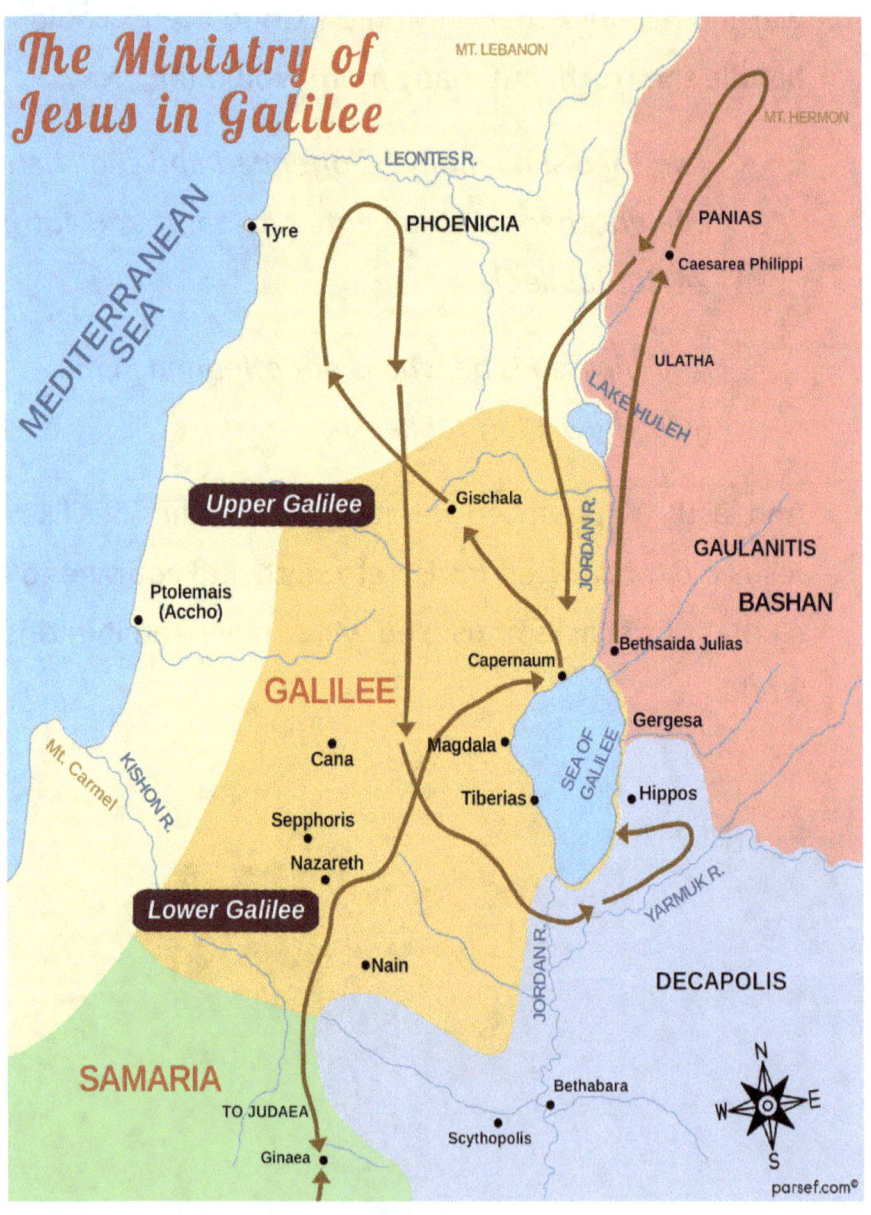

(Bible History Online, 2025)

ABOUT THE AUTHOR

Darnnell Reese is also the author of *Victorious! Defeating Bullies and Giants God's Way. In All Seriousness... Totally Funny Bible Stories* is her second book and is also based on God's Word. Her third book, *Blanket Party in Desert Storm*, will be released soon. The Bible is her weapon of choice to stay far and ahead of the traps and tricks the enemy uses to come against God's children daily. She applies the knowledge and truths It offers to every aspect of her life.

Darnnell believes the Bible is the inspired word of God, and that His word is healing and is life. She also knows laughter is a cure for many pains. And the Bible has an abundance of entertaining stories about a mixed-bag of people who ranged from harmlessly amusing or entertaining to the downright dangerous, unpredictable and even psychotic. To put it mildly, _all_ of them were challenged. But God used them in a mighty way, despite their shortcomings. She skillfully combines God's funny stories, that will make you laugh, with His awesome loving and teachable moments to nourish your soul. Here is your healthy dosage of light hearted humor and God's word, all in one tasty, brightly colored book.

If Darnnell's work has blessed you, she would love to hear from you. Visit her author website at reeseauthor.com for book news, reviews, and ways to connect. A review on Amazon or Goodreads goes a long way — your encouragement truly blesses the author in return.

REFERENCES

(n.d.). Retrieved March 27, 2018, from
https://www.darkmirrors.org/genesis.php

Friedkin, W. (Director). (1973). *The Exorcist* [Motion Picture].

Halliwell , J. O. (1855). Here We Go Round the Mulberry Bush.

Aaron Sorkin, J. M. (Writer), & Becker, H. (Director). (1993). *Malice* [Motion Picture].

Altman, R. (Director). (1980). *Popeye* [Motion Picture].

Ancient-Israel-Old-Testament.html. (n.d.). Retrieved November 28, 2017, from www.bible-history.com/geography

Andrews, T. (Writer), & Nava, G. (Director). (1998). *Why Do Fools Fall In Love* [Motion Picture].

Auburn, D. (Writer), & Madden, J. (Director). (2005). *Proof* [Motion Picture].

August, B. (Director). (1998). *Les Miserables* [Motion Picture].

Avildsen, J., Stallone, S., & Coogler, R. (Directors). (1976-2015). *Rocky Series* [Motion Picture].

Aykroyd, D. (Writer), & Aykroyd, D. (Director). (1991). *Nothing But Trouble* [Motion Picture].

Bain, B. (Writer), & John Krish, P. S. (Director). (1979). *The Jesus Film* [Motion Picture].

Barnz, D. (Director). (2011). *Beastly* [Motion Picture].

Bennet, R. C., & Senensky, R. (Directors). (1978). *Harper Valley PTA* [Motion Picture].

Berry, J. (Director). (1974). *Claudine* [Motion Picture].

Bible History Online. (2025). *Parsef.com.* Retrieved April 11, 2017, from Parsef.com.

Bible Hub. (n.d.). Retrieved January 12, 2018, from http://biblehub.com/commentaries/genesis/38-13.htm: http://biblehub.com/commentaries/genesis/38-13.htm

Blum, J. (Director). (2011). *Savage* [Motion Picture].

Cameron, J. (Writer), & Cameron, J. (Director). (1997). *Titanic* [Motion Picture].

Carson, P. J. (Writer), & Guigui, M. (Director). (2017). *9/11* [Motion Picture].

Court Crandall, T. P. (Writer), & Phillips, T. (Director). (2003). *Old School* [Motion Picture].

Crewe, B., & Nolan, K. (1974). Lady Marmalade [Recorded by Labelle]. On *Nightbirds*.

Crowley, N. (Writer), & Crowley, N. (Director). (2016). *Middle Man* [Motion Picture].

Eastwood, C. (Producer), & Eastwood, C. (Director). (1982). *Firefox* [Motion Picture].

Ellison, R. (1952). *Invisible Man.* Random House.

eutychus-falls-from-a-window. (n.d.). Retrieved March 30, 2018, from https//missionbibleclass.org/1b0-new-testament/new-testament-part-2/acts-epistle-selections/

Face, B. (1994). Water Runs Dry. On *II*. B. Face.

Father Knows Best (TV) (1954-1960). [Motion Picture].

Fay Weldon (novel), B. S. (Writer). (1989). *She-Devil* [Motion Picture].

Filardi, J. (Writer), & Shankman, A. (Director). (2003). *Bringing Down The House* [Motion Picture].

Fleming, V. (Director). (1940). *Gone With The Wind* [Motion Picture].

Fleming, V., Vidor, K., Cukor, G., & Taurog, N. (Directors). (1939). *The Wizard of Oz* [Motion Picture].

Forbes, B. (Director). (1975). *Stepford Wives* [Motion Picture].

Forman, M. (Director). (1975). *One Flew Over the Cuckoo's Nest* [Motion Picture].

Fox, E. (Writer), & Gordon, D. (Director). (2004). *New York Minute* [Motion Picture].

Foxx, R., & Wilson, D. (Performers). (1972-1977). *Sanford and Son.*

Frederick Knott, P. S. (Writer), & Davis, A. (Director). (1998). *A Perfect Murder* [Motion Picture].

Fukasaku, K. (Director). (2000). *Battle Royale* [Motion Picture].

Fusco, J. (Writer), & Murphy, G. (Director). (1988). *Young Guns II* [Motion Picture].

Gibson, M. (Director). (2016). *Hacksaw Ridge* [Motion Picture].

Goddard, G. (Director). (1987). *Masters of the Universe* [Motion Picture].

Gray, F. G. (Director). (1995). *Friday* [Motion Picture].

Hanson, C. (Director). (1992). *The Hand That Rocks the Cradle* [Motion Picture].

Harris, D. (Director). (1991). *Deceived* [Motion Picture].

Haywood, L. (1981). She's A Bad Mama Jama [Recorded by C. Carlton].

Herek, S. (Director). (1996). *101 Dalmatians* [Motion Picture].

Hitchcock, A. (Director). (1960). *Psycho* [Motion Picture].

https://missionbibleclass.org/. (n.d.). Retrieved March 30, 2018, from
https://missionbibleclass.org/: https://missionbibleclass.org/1b0-
new-testament/new-testament-part-2/acts-epistle-
selections/eutychus-falls-from-a-window/

Hughes, J. (Writer), & Hughes, J. (Director). (1987). *Planes Trains and
Automobiles* [Motion Picture].

James L. Brooks, M. G. (Writer), & Silverman, D. (Director). (2007). *The
Simpsons Movie* [Motion Picture].

Jim Carrey, J. D. (Producer), & Farrelly, P. (Director). (1994). *Dumb and
Dumber* [Motion Picture].

Jonah_map2.pdf. (n.d.). Retrieved March 26, 2018, from
https://visualunit.files.wordpress.com/2011/01/

Jovi, J. B. (1990). Blaze of Glory.

Jr., J. L. (Writer), & DeMille, C. B. (Director). (1949). *Samson and Delilah*
[Motion Picture].

Judge, M. (Director). (1996). *Beavis and Butt-Head Do America* [Motion
Picture].

Karl Gajdusek, M. A. (Writer), & Kosinski, J. (Director). (2013). *Oblivion*
[Motion Picture].

Kotcheff, T. (Director). (1983). *Uncommon Valor* [Motion Picture].

Kubrick, S. (Director). (1980). *The Shining* [Motion Picture].

Lancaster, B. (Writer), & Ritchie, M. (Director). (1976). *Bad News Bears*
[Motion Picture].

Lee, A. (Director). (2005). *Brokeback Mountain* [Motion Picture].

Lee, M. D. (Writer), & Lee, M. D. (Director). (1999). *The Best Man* [Motion Picture].

Leon, A. (Writer), & Leon, A. (Director). (2016). *Tramps* [Motion Picture].

LeRoy, M. (Director). (1956). *The Bad Seed* [Motion Picture].

Leterrier, L. (Director). (2008). *The Incredible Hulk* [Motion Picture].

Levant, B. (Director). (1994). *The Flintstones* [Motion Picture].

Lewin, A. (Director). (1945). *The Picture of Dorian Gray* [Motion Picture].

Lewin, A. (Director). (1945). *The Picture of Dorian Gray* [Motion Picture].

Lewis Colick, W. S. (Writer), & Becker, H. (Director). (2001). *Domestic Disturbance* [Motion Picture].

Luc Besson, R. M. (Writer), & Morel, P. (Director). (2008). *Taken* [Motion Picture].

Lucas, G., Kasdan, L. (Writers), & Marquand, R. (Director). (1983). *Star Wars: Return of the Jedi* [Motion Picture].

Lynch, P. (Director). (1989). *Crazy As A Soup Sandwich (TV)* [Motion Picture].

Lyne, A. (Writer), & Dearden, J. (Director). (1987). *Fatal Attraction* [Motion Picture].

Maples, D. (Director). (2008). *In Plain Sight (TV)* [Motion Picture].

Marconi, D. (Writer), & Scott, T. (Director). (1998). *Enemy of the State* [Motion Picture].

Marshall, F. (Director). (1993). *Alive* [Motion Picture].

Marshall, G. (Director). (1957). *The Sad Sack* [Motion Picture].

Matt Lopez, T. H. (Writer), & Shankman, A. (Director). (2008). *Bedtime Stories* [Motion Picture].

Melissa Goddard, A. R. (Writer), & Shea, K. (Director). (1992). *Poison Ivy* [Motion Picture].

Meyer, N. (Director). (1979). *Time After Time* [Motion Picture].

Michael Berry, J. B. (Writer), & Mayfield, L. (Director). (1999). *Blue Streak* [Motion Picture].

Mitch Rotter, S. S. (Writer), & McNamara, S. (Director). (2004). *Raise Your Voice* [Motion Picture].

Obama, M. (n.d.). *National Public Radio*. Retrieved January 16, 2018, from NPR: https://www.npr.org/sections/itsallpolitics/2012/09/04/160581747/michelle-obama-being-president-reveals-who-you-are

O'Jays, T. (1972). Back Stabbers.

Payne, A. (Director). (2004). *Sideways* [Motion Picture].

Pearce, R. (Director). (1999). *Witness Protection* [Motion Picture].

Perry, F. (Director). (1981). *Mommy Dearest* [Motion Picture].

Perry, T. (Director). (2005-2018). *Madea* [Motion Picture].

Peter Wyden, D. W. (Writer), & Sargent, J. (Director). (1989). *Day One* [Motion Picture].

Ritchie, L. (1979). Sail On. Motown.

Robi, R., Child, D., & Escolar, L. G. (1999). Livin' La Vida Loca [Recorded by R. Martin].

Ronald Lang, I. C. (Writer), & Bray, K. (Director). (2002). *All About the Benjamins* [Motion Picture].

Rowell, K. (Writer), & Coppola, F. F. (Director). (1983). *The Outsiders* [Motion Picture].

Sabrina Dhawan, R. O. (Writer), & Rakeysh Omprakash Mehra, J. Z. (Director). (2011). *Bollywood: The Greatest Love Story Ever Told* [Motion Picture]. India.

Sale, R. (Writer), & Allen, L. (Director). (1954). *Suddenly* [Motion Picture].

Samson and the Philistines. (n.d.). Retrieved April 9, 2018, from http://www.headwaterresources.org

Scott Derrickson, C. R. (Writer), & Derrickson, S. (Director). (2012). *Sinister* [Motion Picture].

Seeger, P. (1953). She'll Be Coming 'Round the Mountain [Recorded by P. Seeger].

Shanley, J. P. (Writer), & Shanley, J. P. (Director). (2008). *Doubt* [Motion Picture].

Shapiro, A. (Director). (1978). *Scared Straight* [Motion Picture].

Sheridan, T. (Writer), & Mackenzie, D. (Director). (2016). *Hell or High Water* [Motion Picture].

Silberling, B. (Director). (2004). *Lemony Snicket's A Series of Unfortunate Events* [Motion Picture].

Smith, B. W. (Director). (1992). *BeBe's Kids* [Motion Picture].

Snyder, Z. (Director). (2013). *Man of Steel* [Motion Picture].

Sorkin, A. (Writer), & Reiner, R. (Director). (1992). *A Few Good Men* [Motion Picture].

Stahelski , C., & Leitch, D. (Directors). (2014). *John Wick* [Motion Picture].

Starks, J. B. (1973). The Payback. Polydor.

Stromberg, R. (Director). (2014). *Maleficent* [Motion Picture].

Teague, L. (Director). (1983). *Cujo* [Motion Picture].

Urban Dictionary. (2014). Retrieved December 13, 2017, from
    https://www.urbandictionary.com/define.php?term=bay+bay+kids
    &utm_source=search-action

Vadim, R. (Director). (1968). *Barbarella* [Motion Picture].

Vanderbilt, J. (Writer), & Vanderbilt, J. (Director). (2015). *Truth* [Motion
    Picture].

Wei, L. (Director). (1972). *Fist of Fury* [Motion Picture].

Westlake, D. E. (Writer), & Helgeland, B. (Director). (1999). *Payback*
    [Motion Picture].

Witcher, T. (Writer), & Witcher, T. (Director). (1997). *Love Jones* [Motion
    Picture].

Wright, T. J. (Director). (1989). *No Holds Barred* [Motion Picture].

Zak Penn, S. L. (Writer), & Leterrier, L. (Director). (2008). *The Incredible Hulk*
    [Motion Picture].

Zemeckis, R. (Director). (1994). *Forrest Gump* [Motion Picture].

MOVIE AND TV GUIDE, ENJOY!

Chapter 1
[1] (Harper Valley PTA, 1978)
[2] (Doubt, 2008)
[3] (Crewe & Nolan, 1974)
[4] (Haywood, 1981)
[5] (Malice, 1993)

Chapter 2
[6] (BeBe's Kids, 1992)
[7] (The Bad Seed, 1956)
[8] (Taken, 2008)
[9] (Scared Straight, 1978)
[10] (Nothing But Trouble, 1991)
[11] (Ritchie, 1979)
[12] (Anon., 1972-1977)

Chapter 3
[13] (Lemony Snicket's A Series of Unfortunate Events, 2004)

Chapter 4
[14] (The Exorcist, 1973)
[15] (The Incredible Hulk, 2008)
[16] (Bad News Bears, 1976)
[17] (All About the Benjamins, 2002)
[18] (Blue Streak, 1999)
[19] (Planes Trains and Automobiles, 1987)
[20] (9/11, 2017)

Chapter 5
[21] (The Shining, 1980)
[22] (The Picture of Dorian Gray, 1945)
[23] (Proof, 2005)
[24] (In Plain Sight (TV), 2008)
[25] (Hacksaw Ridge, 2016)
[26] (Crazy As A Soup Sandwich (TV), 1989)
[27] (Alive, 1993)
[28] (Mommy Dearest, 1981)
[29] (Father Knows Best (TV), 1954-1960)
[30] (Robi, et al., 1999)
[31] (One Flew Over the Cuckoo's Nest, 1975)
[32] (Cujo, 1983)

Chapter 6
[33] (Friday, 1995)

Chapter 7
[34] (Barbarella, 1968)
[35] (Star Wars: Return of the Jedi, 1983)
[36] (Love Jones, 1997)
[37] (A Perfect Murder, 1998)
[38] (Sinister, 2012)

Chapter 8
[39] (O'Jays, 1972)
[40] (The Hand That Rocks the Cradle, 1992)
[41] (Claudine, 1974)

Chapter 9

[42] (Maleficent, 2014)

[43] (The Wizard of Oz, 1939)

[44] (Witness Protection, 1999)

[45] (Face, 1994)

[46] (Les Miserables, 1998)

[47] (Man of Steel, 2013)

[48] (Dumb and Dumber, 1994)

[49] (101 Dalmatians, 1996)

[50] (Rocky Series, 1976-2015)

Chapter 10

[51] (The Sad Sack, 1957)

[52] (Suddenly, 1954)

[53] (Beavis and Butt-Head Do America, 1996)

[54] (Popeye, 1980)

[55] (Brokeback Mountain, 2005)

[56] (John Wick, 2014)

[57] (Battle Royale, 2000)

[58] (Forrest Gump, 1994)

Chapter 11

[59] (Time After Time, 1979)

[60] (The Incredible Hulk, 2008)

[61] (Masters of the Universe, 1987)

[62] (The Flintstones, 1994)

[63] (Sideways, 2004)

Chapter 12

[64] (Deceived, 1991)

[65] (Psycho, 1960)
[66] (Savage, 2011)
[54](Day One, 1989)
[68] (Firefox, 1982)
[69] (Beastly, 2011)
[70] (No Holds Barred, 1989)
[71] (Old School, 2003)
[72] (Uncommon Valor, 1983)
[73] (Fist of Fury, 1972)
[74] (Starks, 1973)
[75] (Payback, 1999)
[76] (Why Do Fools Fall In Love, 1998)
[77] (Samson and Delilah, 1949)
[78] (Poison Ivy, 1992)
[79] (Bedtime Stories, 2008)
[80] (New York Minute, 2004)
[81] (She-Devil, 1989)
[82] (Sinister, 2012)
[83] (Bringing Down The House, 2003)
[84] (Young Guns II, 1988)
[85] (Jovi, 1990)
[86] (The Best Man, 1999)

Chapter 13
[87] (The Outsiders, 1983)
[88] (Oblivion, 2013)
[89] (Domestic Disturbance, 2001)
[90] (Tramps, 2016)
[91] (Fatal Attraction, 1987)
[92] (Hell or High Water, 2016)
[93] (Madea, 2005-2018)

---

[94] (Raise Your Voice, 2004)

Chapter 14
[95] (Truth, 2015)
[96] (Enemy of the State, 1998)
[97] (The Jesus Film, 1979)
[98] (Titanic, 1997)
[99] (A Few Good Men, 1992)